African
Hats and Jewelry

African
Hats and Jewelry

DUNCAN CLARKE

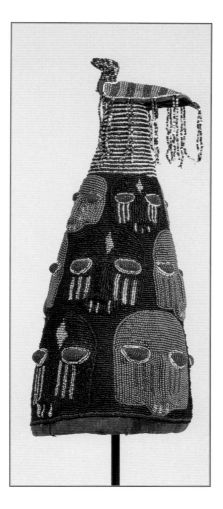

CHARTWELL
BOOKS, INC.

This edition published in 1998 by
CHARTWELL BOOKS, INC.
A division of BOOK SALES, INC
114 Northfield Avenue,
Edison, New Jersey 08837

Produced by PRC Publishing Ltd,
Kiln House, 210 New Kings Road, London SW6 4NZ

© 1998 PRC Publishing Ltd.

ISBN 0 78580 984 8

Printed and bound in China

CONTENTS

INTRODUCTION

From the intricate and precious jewels of the pharaohs of ancient Egypt to the stark simplicity of a worn ivory bracelet, from the complex multi-colored silk designs of Asante kente cloths to the black and white mudcloth bogolan of Mali, African style has intrigued and enthralled the world. Earlier this century great innovative artists such as Pablo Picasso, Henri Matisse, and Paul Klee drew new forms and devised vibrant color combinations from the arts of Africa. Today fashion designers as diverse as Donna Karan and John Galliano have looked to Africa for inspiration. Decorating and adorning the human body is a vital component of the visual arts in Africa that continues to display extraordinary vitality in the face of far-reaching social change.

The West African kingdom of Asante—in the modern state of Ghana—became famous in the 19th century for the fabled splendor of its royal court. Best known today as the source of kente cloth, the extravagant style of Asante court life was first revealed to a European audience by T.E. Bowdich who visited the capital Kumase in 1817. In his book, *Mission from Cape Coast Castle to Ashantee*, Bowdich described their reception:

"The sun was reflected, with a glare scarcely more supportable than the heat, from the massy gold ornaments, which glistened in every direction . . . At least 100 large umbrellas, or canopies, which could shelter 30 persons, were sprung up and down by the bearers with brilliant effect. The caboceers as did their superior captains and attendants, wore Ashantee cloths of extravagant price . . . they were of incredible size and weight, and thrown over their shoulder exactly like a Roman toga; a small silk fillet generally encircled their temples, and massy gold necklaces, intricately wrought; suspended Moorish charms . . . a band of gold and beads encircled the knee, from which several strings of the same depended; small circles of gold like guineas, rings, and casts of animals, were strung around their ankles; their sandles [sic] were of green, red and delicate white leather; manillas and rude lumps of rock gold hung from their left wrists, which were so heavily laden as to be supported on the head of one of their handsomest boys. Gold and silver pipes, and canes dazzled the eye in every direction."

ABOVE: Elaborate scarification patterns of the type worn by this Kongo woman were discontinued after the early decades of the 20th century. They were regarded as a mark of her bravery as well as an enhancement of beauty. Similar patterns were reproduced on textiles and sculpture dating back over several centuries.

RIGHT: A painting depicting Igbo women's ceremonial costume of "olden days" (ekike ndi gboo) including ivory anklets, beads, and uli body decorations. Earth pigments on clay wall, Nnobi, Nigeria, 1987.

Although the political power of the Asante has been much reduced in the 20th century, their king, the Asantehene, is still capable of mounting similar displays of wealth, parading in gold jewelry and silk cloths on state occasions—such as the 25th anniversary of the reign of the current ruler Otumfuo Opoku Ware II in 1995.

In the harsh desert scrublands of Namibia and South Africa small bands of San hunter-gather-

ers still laboriously fashion jewelry by carefully grinding ostrich eggshells to form tiny disc-shaped beads, which are sewn to the fringes of leather garments. Necklaces and bracelets—made in exactly the same fashion as they have been for thousands of years—from carefully matched seeds and tiny bones, are today supplemented with those woven from brightly-colored electric wires stripped from isolated telephone posts.

Thousands of miles and a huge gulf in material wealth separate these two African peoples, yet they are united in their appreciation of the arts of body decoration. Throughout Africa people have displayed, and continue to display, an extraordinary flair and creativity in dressing and adorning their bodies. This book recognizes and celebrates that creativity through an introduction to the art and style of African adornment as displayed in jewelry, beadwork, hats, clothing, and

ABOVE (DETAIL) AND LEFT: *A contemporary version of Igbo uli body painting tradition, executed in eyebrow pencil on a member of the Odumgbede dance group at Arochukwu, Nigeria, 1994.*

masquerade. It explores some of the ways in which, using an incredible range of both local and imported materials, African peoples have expressed and portrayed ideas about such concerns as status and identity, modesty and decorum, wealth and power, beauty and love, fashion and tradition, protection and healing. It illustrates the use of the arts of body adornment in the construction of social relations, helping to transform biological entities into fully social community participants, and even, in the case of masks and masquerade, into representations of extra-social spiritual entities.

Africa is a vast continent inhabited by several hundred million people speaking a huge range of languages and with cultures adapted to life in a wide diversity of environments—everything from tropical rainforests to the fringes of some of the world's harshest deserts. Historians have now recognized that their earlier image of time-

less, unchanging tribal cultures shattered forever by the shock of their conquest by civilizing Europeans was an aspect of the same racist denigration of non-European peoples that was used in justification of colonization, and before that of the slave trade. Colonial rule, established in most areas only at the start of the 20th century and drawing to a close by the 1960s, was only a comparatively brief, if generally unwelcome, interval in long histories that were marked by foreign interventions. Such disruptions included not only the impact of world religions, as well as both Arab and European slave trades, but also locally initiated changes—from the spread of new crops and of metal working techniques to the effects of trade, wars, and population movements. The styles of dress, headgear, jewelry, and masquerade attire discussed and illustrated in this volume, arise out of a few of these diverse local histories and circumstances, even if in most cases we lack sufficient information to be able to reconstruct these histories in any depth or detail. Although some of these modes may have appeared to change little for decades, or even hundreds of years, others were subject to rapidly changing fashions, the subtlety of which was often lost on the occasional overseas observer.

African arts were not, as we often think, static unchanging traditional forms that endlessly reproduced tribal styles. Rather they were—and in many cases still are—living and evolving traditions in which creativity and individual initiative play a key role alongside the forms handed on from the past. The 20th century has been a period of particularly rapid and far-reaching change in many parts of Africa; like all change this has involved both gains and losses. Amongst the losses have been the drastic modification or even abandonment of many of the forms of dress

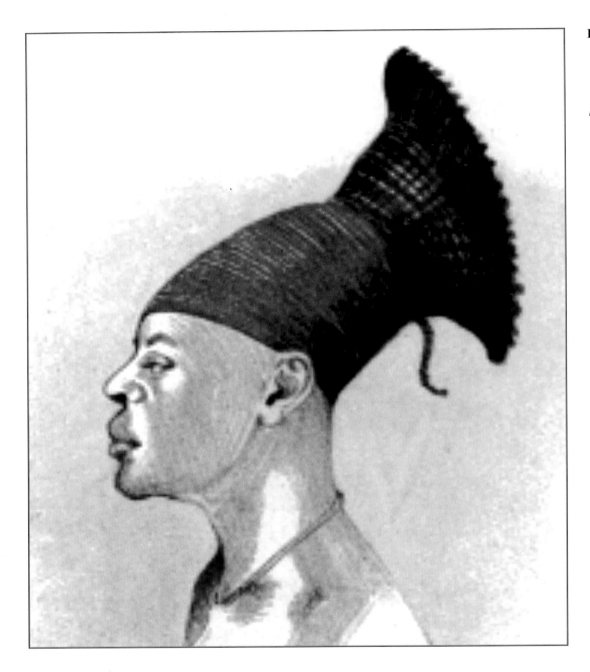

LEFT AND BELOW RIGHT: *Mangbetu women in the northeast of Congo (formerly Zaire) bound the skulls of young babies to produce an elongated head shape, an effect that was emphasized in adults by weaving the hair around a circular basketry frame. Sketch made by E.M. Heims on the German Central African Expedition of 1910-11.*

and adornment that were popular in the past. In some cases these changes were in part enforced ones, imposed by missionaries, colonial, or even post-colonial governments. In many others they were voluntarily embraced by people keen to take advantage of new possibilities and opportunities in the modern world. In still others, forms of attire which are thought of as traditional, were in fact adopted quite recently as people have found it to their advantage in changing circumstances to dress in ways that stress a new sense of group identity. To dismiss these changes is to expect other peoples to fossilize their lifestyles simply to provide an exotic spectacle for tourists and photographers. Instead they adapt, modify, incorporate new materials, and new influences, select things from the past to continue and others to abandon, while still seeking to express through their bodies a wide range of human concerns.

Most of this book will be concerned with the artefacts created in these processes, with jewelry, beads, hats, cloths, and masks. Other key aspects of African style however, involve the direct decoration of the body itself by modifying the body surface and arranging of hair styles. If many of the forms and styles of this mode of African adornment may appear particularly exotic and even bizarre, we should recall that modifying the surface appearance and shape of the human body are among the oldest inclinations of mankind, and such endeavors have become well established in the contemporary culture of America. We need think only of make-up, dieting, cosmetic surgery, body building, or tattooing.

Except among the Berber peoples of the mountains of North Africa, true tattooing—which involves the insertion of pigments into the skin—is rarely found in Africa, probably because the technique has little visual impact on dark skin. Instead, in many areas of the continent, the practice known as cicatrization has been popu-

RIGHT: *Young women of the pastoral Fulani are a common sight in the markets of many West African towns, selling milk and cheese from finely decorated calabashes. Even for everyday dress they frequently create elaborate and extraordinary hairstyles such as this, while the patterns of tattoos on their face and bodies are expanded progressively from childhood. Bida, Nigeria, 1995.*

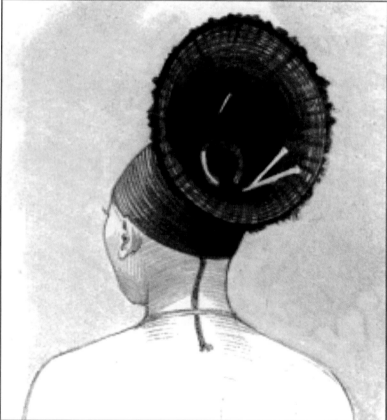

lar. This involves cutting the skin so that it heals to form decorative patterns. There are various types ranging from the patterns of short, thin cuts known as *kolo* among the Yoruba of Nigeria, to the designs of small raised lumps, or keloids, formed by raising tiny sections of skin and inserting an irritant, such as ash, beneath. Tools used include razor blades, tiny iron knives, nails, and thorns. In some cultures a full set of designs was regarded as essential to a well-formed adult. Beginning in some cases soon after birth, designs may be added at various important stages in the child's life, such as at circumcision, puberty, and initiation into a society, visibly marking off the progress towards adulthood. Sometimes particular designs held a specific symbolism, in others they were purely decorative. Often the designs cut on women's bodies would also be used in other female arts such as pottery decoration, calabash carving, or the painting of the walls of house compounds and granaries. Sculptures and old photographs provide a fascinating record of patterns of cicatrization that have now been abandoned in many areas.

Other forms of permanent body modification that were much less widely distributed included enlarging the lower lip through the insertion of progressively larger lip plates or labrets, as among the Kichepo of Sudan and the Sara of southern Chad; the gradual stretching of the neck by large beaded neck-rings among some Ndebele in South Africa; and the slight modification of the shape of the head. The Mangbetu of northeast Congo (formerly Zaire) achieved a long slender head shape by binding the top of babies' heads, while Asante royalty preferred an even, rounded face, which mothers sought to achieve by smoothing out their child's face. This ideal is depicted in exaggerated form in the flat disc-shaped heads of the little akua'ba dolls Asante women carried to help them conceive well-formed babies.

More temporary forms of body decoration, especially painting, was often used to mark out individuals in transitional or liminal states, such as youths in long initiation camps being instructed in the knowledge necessary to progress to adulthood. Girls undergoing initiation by women elders of the Sande society among groups such as the Mende and Vai of Sierra Leone and Liberia, paraded in the village with their bodies gleaming with oil, or painted in chalk patterns. In Nigeria, among the Igbo people, designs known as *uli*, also used by women in wall-painting, were painted onto young girls on festive occasions, using a plant extract which had a dark blue color. Young Maasai girls recovering from their circumcision dress very drably and paint their faces with chalk for a six-week period. For Maasai men the transition from warriors to elders involves both body painting and a dramatic change in hairstyle and jewelry. As warriors they have spent years preoccupied with their appearance, working every day on more elaborate hairstyles and jewelry, so marking their achievements and attracting lovers. At the festival that ends this period of their lives, they dress in this finery for a final few days, often painting their bodies in elaborate chalk designs, before the ritual shaving of their head by their mothers marks their assumption of the more constrained life of an elder, when they must marry and participate in the responsibilities of leadership.

As the Maasai example suggests, hairstyles are

ABOVE: *Yoruba young women's hairstyles from the 1950s.*

RIGHT: *In urban communities the aspirations to western dress and lifestyles prompted by access to imported magazines and television find expression in a thriving art of sign painting, particularly those such as this advertising a barber's shop. Ibadan, Nigeria, 1997.*

also crucial markers of status in many African societies. Chiefs and elders often had distinctive hairstyles, while among women hairstyles might distinguish between young girls, those of marriageable status, those already married, and, in some cases, even widows. Unusually, among the Yoruba, male priests of the thunder god Sango adopted the clothes and the hairstyle of young brides to indicate their role as brides of the deity.

Until early this century, married Zulu women used animal fat mixed with ochre to form a circular column of hair, weaving in grass to add bulk, while married men wove their hair around a fiber head-ring or *isicoco*. Where elaborate and long-lasting hairstyles were important, men in particular, used a small wooden headrest to support their head off the ground while they slept.

As with all forms of body adornment, fashions in hairstyles changed periodically. By the 1950s international styles—particularly those favored by prominent and admired African-American sportsmen such as boxer Muhammed Ali—became very influential in urban areas throughout Africa. Local painters were enlisted to illustrate these aspirational styles on signs displayed outside barber shops and salons, as illustrated on page 15. By the late 1990s the more naive images were being replaced in some cities by increasingly polished copies of magazine advertisements depicting contemporary aspirations for Western fashion.

JEWELRY IN AFRICA

ADORNMENT, WEALTH, AND STATUS

Jewelry in Africa, as elsewhere, is all about beauty and display, about men and women looking elegant, wealthy, and appropriately adorned. Beyond this, however, are issues of rank and status, in which jewelry—like the body decorations, hairstyles, hats, clothing and other items of attire we will explore elsewhere in this book—functions to construct and signify aspects of the social role of the wearer within his or her community. From pharaohs, kings, and chiefs, to humble farmers and hunters, aspects of jewelry were associated with marking hierarchies and distinctions: between royalty and commoners; rich and poor; men and women; initiates and non-initiates; locals and strangers; adults and youths.

ABOVE AND RIGHT: Ivory armlets were much prized heirlooms, often taking on a smooth reddish patina from repeated rubbing with palm oil. Above is a Hausa armlet from Nigeria. The others are, clockwise from top: Songye (Congo), Edo (Nigeria), and Dinka (Sudan).

At the same time, in cultures that generally did not recognize individual ownership of land, jewelry was and still remains one of the most important ways in which wealth could be accumulated and passed on to future generations. This was particularly important for women, since in many societies other forms of transferable wealth were usually exclusively in the hands of men. Jewelry, as a major component of bodily adornment, was also frequently a medium through which aspects of socially important symbolic ideas could be explored. These general themes often recur in different expressions throughout the myriad approaches adopted over the centuries by the diverse cultures that have developed throughout the African continent. Such themes are conditioned as much by differing aesthetic sensibilities, the accidents of history, political and social organizations, and religious beliefs, as by access to both local and imported techniques and materials. In the following chapter we will look at the many uses of beads and bead-work in African jewelry, while here we will concentrate on the use of metals, ivory, and precious stones.

Ancient Egyptian kings, queens, and nobles were adorned with jewels fashioned in great state-run workshops, several of which have been recorded on surviving wall-paintings and stone reliefs. Depictions of jewelry in the portraits of

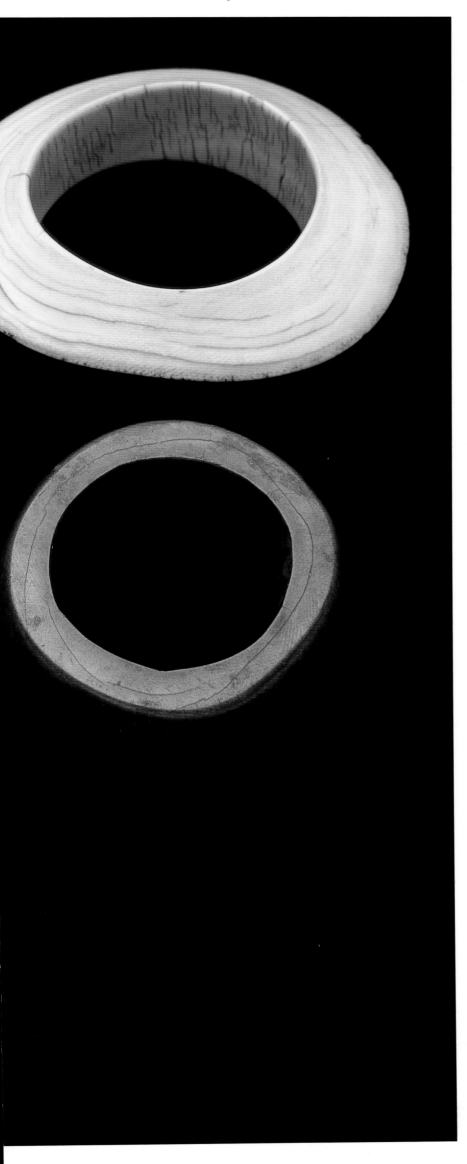

both mortals and gods on the walls of tombs, as well as treasuries of the jewels themselves uncovered in tombs and pyramids have provided scholars with detailed information on the splendor and variety of Egyptian craftsmanship. The jewelers of the state workshops fashioned bracelets, anklets, armbands, necklaces, pendants, pectoral ornaments, crowns, and diadems, using a huge range of materials. Although gold was the most widely used metal, copper was especially important in early jewelry, being used for rings and bangles even in the Predynastic period. Interestingly, silver was more precious than gold, since it was not available locally and had to be obtained through trade or as war booty from Asia Minor; furthermore it was believed that the bones of the gods were made of silver. Faïence, a glazed material made from firing certain types of powdered quartz, sand, and glass were frequently used, as were a wide range of stones including agate, amethyst, garnet, jade, and blue lapis lazuli. Ivory was among the most significant of Egypt's imports from areas of Africa to the south, in particular from the lands of Nubia and Punt.

Although some Egyptian jewelry was purely decorative, most had additional significance as insignia of rank and as protective amulets. The most important jewels would accompany the deceased into the grave, where they would be supplemented by numerous additional items intended to provide special protection for the deceased in the difficult transition to the afterlife. As with many other aspects of ancient Egyptian art, the design of jewelry incorporated many hieroglyphs, allowing the symbolic meaning of most pieces to be literally decoded. Egyptian writing utilized a system of hieroglyphs—standardized pictures—that both conveyed a recognized meaning in themselves and could be combined to form units like syllables in longer words. Among the more important hieroglyphs that frequently occurred in jewelry were the Wedjat eye and the ankh. The Wedjat eye represents the moon in the form of the left eye of

LEFT: *Selection of ivory armlets: top left Shiluk (Sudan); bottom right Gurunsi (Ghana); center (left to right) Igbo, Edo, Yoruba (all Nigeria).*

19

the great falcon god Horus, with the waxing and waning of the moon associated with a story of the healing of the god's damaged eye. In jewelry and other art it serves as both a protective device and a symbol of offering, recalling Horus's presentation of the restored eye to his father. The ankh, the cross form with a loop at the top, which has now become a widely used symbol of Afrocentricity, was the symbol for life and the breath of life, and for the vital properties of both air and water.

Although scholars still dispute whether the direct influence of Egypt was extended in sub-Saharan Africa much more widely than its southern neighbors in the various kingdoms of Nubia, it is clear that there have been frequent contacts across the expanse now occupied by the Sahara for several thousand years. Trade goods and a variety of cultural influences were exchanged in both directions along routes still marked by ancient rock paintings of horses and chariots. Although there is little securely dated ancient jewelry from most regions of sub-Saharan Africa, evidence of sophisticated metalworking techniques and some jewelry has been recovered from finds such as Igbo Ukwu in southeastern Nigeria (dated to around the 9th century) and large quantities of gold and copper alloy jewelry were looted from unscientific excavations at Great Zimbabwe and related sites in the southern part of the continent. Evidence of ancient jewelry also survives in the form of bracelets, necklaces, etc, depicted on the terracotta figures from the vicinity of ancient Jenne in Mali, Bura in Niger, and the Nok culture in Nigeria, as well as the copper alloy cast figures of ancient Ife (12th to 15th century) and Benin (14th century to date).

When Mansa Musa, king of the ancient empire of Mali made the pilgrimage to Mecca in 1324–25 he crossed the Sahara with a convoy of at least 10,000 retainers, bringing with him so much gold that the value of the metal was depressed in Cairo for many years afterwards. Gold, along with slaves and ivory, were to form the major

African exports for many centuries, both by caravans across the desert and in seaborne trade with Arabs along the eastern coast, and from the late 15th century, with Europeans along the west. In Africa itself however, gold was only available for use as jewelry in a quite limited number of areas, and in some places was not as highly valued as copper. Gold jewelry, including a small gold-plated model of a rhinoceros, has been excavated from burial sites at Mapungubwe, a hill-top settlement thought to be the capital of a state that flourished in the Limpopo river basin in southeast Africa between the 11th and 12th centuries. More recently the use of gold jewelry is particularly associated with the Akan peoples of Ghana and Côte D'Ivoire, with the Tukolor and Wolof of Senegal, and with wealthier sections of the nomadic Fulani in countries such as Mali.

Techniques used in the manufacture of gold jewelry include gold-plating of wooden objects, engraving, hammering and chasing, filigree and granulation, and lost-wax casting. This latter is important both in gold-smithing and in the far more widespread use of brass and other copper alloys. It involves making a finely detailed model of the desired object using beeswax or various types of latex. This model is then gradually coated in clay, starting with a very fine, smooth layer and building it up little by little until the model is encased in a solid dry casing. The casing is then heated until the wax melts, running out of a channel, leaving a clay mold into which molten metal is poured. Once the metal has cooled the mold can be broken and the object smoothed and finished.

Gold dust was used as currency in the Asante empire in 18th and 19th century Ghana, and the key symbol of Asante power to this day is the Golden Stool, to which are attached cast gold effigies representing conquered enemies. It is thought that most goldsmiths in the Asante capital of Kamase were descendants of skilled craftsmen from the states of Denkyira and Takyiman, captured when the Asante defeated their predecessors as regional powers. Gold jewelry was an important item in the regalia of senior chiefs and royal permission was needed before certain major types could be commissioned. Among the

LEFT: *Igbo woman from the Onitsha region of Nigeria wearing the huge coral beads, white cloth, and thick ivory bracelets and anklets indicating that she has taken the prestigious and expensive Ozo title. The bands of cotton round her wrists serve to lessen the discomfort of such heavy regalia. This is a 1960s view.*

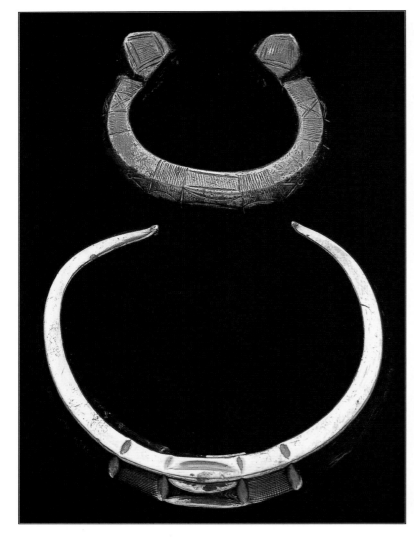

ABOVE: *Brass collar and armlet worn by Fang women in northern Gabon.*

RIGHT: *Brass was a highly prestigious material throughout much of West and Central Africa, fashioned into a wide variety of necklaces, bracelets and anklets.*

gold ornaments worn by Asante are bracelets, circular pectoral insignia for palace servants, rings, necklaces, sandal decorations, and royal crowns. Many of these (like the small brass casts used for weighing gold dust), include depictions of birds, animals, the heads of slain enemies, and references to proverbs. Similar gold jewelry made by the technique of lost-wax casting, often supplemented by filigree surface decoration, is also found amongst other Akan peoples such as the Baule.

Senegalese gold jewelry combines aspects similar to the Akan style with influences from North Africa and the Mediterranean. For women of the Tukolor and Wolof, elaborate gold jewelry is both an important means of enhancing and displaying their beauty and also a key store of wealth. One popular form, associated with jewelers of the Tukolor, is a bi-conical-shaped pendant, called a corval. According to the French researcher Dominique Zahan, the shape

represents a weaver's bobbin with the dependence of the ornament on its leather cord being a symbol of the control of the husband over his wife. In contrast to the complex ornamentation of Senegalese gold working, wealthy Fulani women in the Malian towns of Jenne and Mopti, wear huge but simple gold earrings, made by hammering bars of solid gold into thin twisted blades.

Although silver is used for jewelry in some areas of West Africa it is particularly associated with the Tuareg of the Sahara and the peoples of eastern Africa. At the time of marriage a Tuareg groom should give his wife a collection of silver jewelry, including a pair of large earrings, a ring-shaped pendant, two types of crosses, a necklace with a third cross shape, and a long complex ornament used for weighting the back of her head cloth. The numerous cross forms in Tuareg jewelry are not thought to have Christian origins, but their precise symbolism is unknown. Silver amulet cases containing passages from the *Koran* are also an important aspect of Tuareg jewelry. Most Tuareg jewelry is made by a separate caste of smiths that combines claims to Jewish north African ancestry with the legacy of incorporating countless generations of slave women from the south.

The silver jewelry of much of the eastern African coast reflects many hundreds of years of involvement by both Somali and Swahili-speaking peoples with Arabia and the Arab-dominated trading networks of the Indian Ocean. More distinctive forms have, however, developed in the highlands of Ethiopia. The Ethiopian kingdom of Axum was converted to Christianity in 330AD, and Christian iconography has remained a key feature of the arts of the region. In the 15th century the Emperor Zara Yacob (1434–1468) decreed that all his subjects should wear a cross. Since that time crosses have become the dominant form in Ethiopian jewelry, although beads, rings, and other pendants are also made. Some very early crosses made from wood or gold still survive in museum collections, but since the 18th century most have been made of silver. Silver was imported into Africa in large quantities after 1740 in the form of Austrian coins known as Maria Theresa thaler (the source of the name dollar). A wide repertoire of intricate elaborations on the basic cross form have been developed.

Brass and other copper alloys were much more widely available in sub-Saharan Africa and have long been prized for their red lustre and ease of working. Using the techniques of lost-wax casting, or in some areas more simple molds, hammering of molten metal, and drawing of cop-

RIGHT: *The small brass double figure pendants worn by both the Senufo of Ivory Coast (left) and the Dogon of Mali (center and right) allude respectively to primordial ancestors and to mythological twins.*

BELOW RIGHT: *Iron and stone dugo necklace worn perhaps by a priest or hogon, or by an ordinary individual of the Dogon people (Mali). Dugo are worn as a sign connecting the wearer to an immediate ancestor or some other spiritual entity important to them. In the case of hogon, this may be the mythical ancestor Lebe.*

per wire, a huge range of jewelry such as bracelets, rings, necklaces, and anklets have been manufactured, both for everyday use and for court and ritual regalia. Here we will consider two examples drawn from widely separated areas of the continent, namely the Senufo peoples of Côte D'Ivoire and the Zulu of South Africa.

Among the Senufo brass ornaments are worn as protective charms or amulets, called *yawiige*, following the instructions of a female diviner. According to the American anthropologist Anita Glaze they are intended to appease potentially hostile and dangerous bush spirits who might otherwise threaten the health and prosperity of the wearer. The diviner herself would use numerous small figurative castings in exploring her clients problems. Bracelets, anklets, and rings were cast with the form of a wide range of animals associated with the bush spirits, with smaller versions made for children. Pythons and chameleons are particularly important images often found on women's bracelets and men's rings, reflecting their prominence in Senufo myth and symbolic thought. Brass rings with the head and sweeping horns of the bushcow were worn only by members of an association of healers as a sign of their office.

ABOVE: *A late 19th century photograph of a north African woman of Arab descent.*

RIGHT: *Tuareg silver jewelry. In the center are tcherot, copper-decorated silver boxes containing protective verses from the Koran or related magic formulae. On the right and left are assrou n'swoul, pendants worn at the back as counterweights to hold in place women's headcloths.*

In 19th century South Africa copper was a rare and prestigious metal bought from Europeans. Among the Zulu its use was highly restricted and controlled by the royal court. Copper was cast into clay molds by smiths working to the orders of the king, who rewarded them with gifts of cattle. There were two types of neck rings: the first was a flat ring of solid brass worn only by chiefs; the second, a tubular ring used by senior men and women. This broad band had a notched surface, and was worn around the forearm, its use was restricted to the king and certain senior advisors and warriors, while the wearing of brass studs on leather skirts was reserved for the wives of the king and senior chiefs. Although the latter became far more

widely available later in the century the restrictions on many types of brass jewelry continued despite the British defeat of the Zulu kings.

In the kingdom of Benin, in southern Nigeria, a similar elaborate system of restrictions and sumptuary laws controlled the use of a wide range of regalia. The king granted favored individuals the right to wear coral beads, while brass regalia was reserved for chiefs. The king himself wore similar items of regalia made instead from ivory. As in many other parts of Africa, the rarity and expense of ivory, together with its association with the elephant, the most powerful and dangerous of animals, made it a material suited

LEFT: *Ivory jewelry (left to right): Pende ikhoko pendant in the form of a mask, initially worn by young man to protect the owner during the dangerous period of initiation into adulthood, Congo; Lega pendant, Congo; Turkana labret or lip plug, Kenya.*

BELOW: *Zulu earplugs called amashaza, made from a wooden disc covered with section cut from plastic floor tiles. They were popular presents brought home by migrant laborers for their wives during the 1950s.*

RIGHT: *Necklace attributed to the Baule of central Ivory Coast, strung with numerous brass beads, each separately cast using the lost wax technique.*

LEFT: *Dinka segmented ivory bracelet, afiok, thought to be worn by young women of marriageable age.*

BELOW LEFT: *Nigerian early 20th century brass bracelet worn by officials of the Yoruba ogboni cult, depicting a man with legs turning into mudfish. The mudfish, which could move between water and land, was a widely used symbol of anomalous powers that transgressed normal boundaries, and therefore appropriate for the society of elders with occult powers.*

RIGHT: *Brass mask in the form of a leopard's head, worn on the hip by a Benin chief as part of a ceremonial outfit. Only the king was entitled to wear similar ivory hip-masks.*

to the manufacture of jewelry for only the most senior and powerful of individuals. Among the Igbo of Nigeria senior titled women displayed their wealth and status by the use of thick ivory bracelets, and anklets that encircled their legs almost to the knees.

Although as we have seen, jewelry in Africa has played its part in representing hierarchies of rank, wealth, and status, and has implications for a variety of social and religious roles, we should not lose sight of the fact that it is also inextricably concerned in most cases with issues of beauty and appropriate display. As such it has not become set in unchanging tribal styles. Although we can easily identify only the many changes and often losses of the recent past, it is likely that previous periods were also characterized by changing fashions and tastes. As long ago as the 1850s an American missionary, William Clarke, observed a Yoruba jeweler altering the shape of a number of copper rings. In response to his questions the craftsman told him that a woman had brought them in to have them reworked into the latest style, prompting him to comment that, "these little trinkets undergo their changes according to fashion, just as the cut of a coat or the trimming of a bonnet on Broadway."

ABOVE: *A Somali couple pictured in the late 19th century.*

RIGHT: *Necklace of silver, coins, and imported beads, from the Harer region of Somalia.*

OVERLEAF: *Hammered brass ogba anklet, one of a pair worn by young Igbo women. Since they were both extremely expensive and prevented the wearer from working actively, these bracelets enhanced the prestige of the wearer and her husband.*

BEADS AND BEADWORK

Archaeological research has demonstrated that beads and beadwork have played a prominent role throughout the long history of jewelry and adornment in Africa. The first evidence comes with beads made from ground discs of ostrich eggshell, dated to around 10,000BC, discovered in Sudan and Libya. Very similar beads are still made using the same technique by San hunter-gatherers in Botswana. Beads from Rome and Ptolemaic Egypt have been excavated in the ancient Malian town of Jenne, at sites dated to between 300BC and 200AD, providing the earliest evidence of the long-standing trade in imported beads in sub-Saharan Africa. Evidence of the extent of these trade routes is provided by the discovery of over a hundred thousand glass and carnelian beads in a royal burial chamber dated to around the 9th century, along with numerous sophisticated bronze castings, at Igbo Ukwu in southeastern Nigeria. Some of these beads are thought to be from Europe, some probably from India or the Middle East, while others are likely to be of more local origin. At Ife—according to legend the center for kingship among the Yoruba of Nigeria—there is evidence as early as the 8th century that imported European glass beads were being melted down and reworked into local designs.

ABOVE AND RIGHT: *Only those Yoruba kings who can sustain a claim to descent from Oduduwa, the legendary ruler of the sacred city of Ife, are entitled to wear a beaded crown.*

As with the metal and ivory jewelry already discussed, beads and beadwork have been, and in some areas still are, intimately involved in a huge variety of aspects of social life in numerous African cultures. They are used in displaying beauty, wealth, or rank, for protection and healing, to mark religious affiliation, as signs of life-cycle stages, and as indicators of group identity. Beads in the form of a simple loop around the waist are frequently the first item of dress any child will receive. In this chapter we will explore some facets of the multiple roles played by beads in African adornment through a brief account of their use in some of the societies of western, eastern, and southern Africa.

Although we will concentrate mostly on glass beads, a huge range of other substances have been used in local beadwork manufacture throughout the continent.

Ostrich eggshells were used for jewelry in many regions, as were the shells of large snails and of mollusks where available. Many types of small seed could be made into beads by drilling a hole through them. Small bones, including snake vertebrae, were a popular source of beads, as were the teeth of prestigious animals such as lions and leopards; these latter were usually the preserve of chiefs and senior warriors. Metal beads were

manufactured throughout Africa, using gold, silver, brass, iron, and more recently aluminum. Both clay and wood have been used to make beads; more exotically, amber from the Baltic coast of northern Europe has long been a popular bead material across the Sahel, and in Ethiopia, and Somalia, while copal amber from Mozambique and Zanzibar is widely found throughout the same areas. The ethnologist and bead expert, Margaret Carey, has noted that several peoples make fragrant-smelling beads, including the Kikuyu of Kenya who use rolled-up leaves and small dried vegetable tubers, and the Sotho of Lesotho who add vegetable perfume to small balls of clay. A wide variety of stones could also be laboriously ground into shape to form

beads, of which the red agate and jasper lantana beads of Ilorin and Bida are the best known. Imported plastic beads have become a cheaper substitute for glass over the past 40 years or so.

The vast majority of glass beads used in Africa have been imported from elsewhere; apart from the glassworks of ancient Egypt and the Arab craftsmen of North African towns, there are very few sites in Africa where the techniques of glassmaking were known. Although glass bead-making crucibles have been discovered at Ife, many scholars feel that the evidence suggests these were for re-working imported glass, not local manufacture as such. The only well-documented evidence for indigenous glass-making in sub-Saharan Africa comes from the Nupe capital of

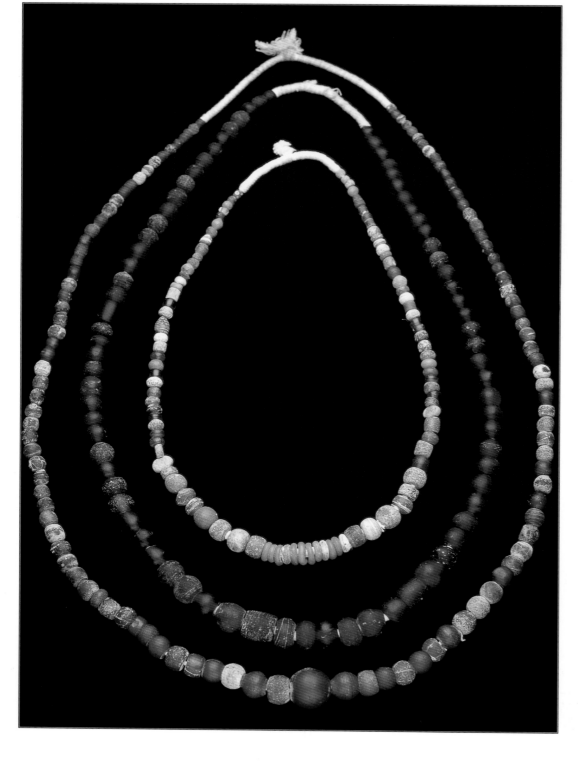

LEFT: *Ancient glass beads of European origin, recovered from looted tombs in the inland Niger delta region of Mali.*

TOP RIGHT: *Clay spindle whorls for spinning cotton thread re-used as beads, Dogon region, Mali.*

BOTTOM FAR RIGHT: *Necklace of rough quartz beads from the Dogon region of Mali.*

RIGHT: *Mandja woman dressed for the Samali festival, culmination of a three-month period of initiation. Her outfit combines cowrie shells with imported red, blue, and white glass beads. This is a 1910 photograph taken in the Central African Republic.*

40

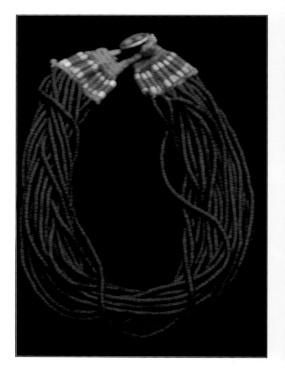

TOP: *Ostrich shell bead necklace of the Turkana people.*

ABOVE: *Multi-stranded necklace of Venetian glass beads worn by Dinka pastoralists of southern Sudan.*

RIGHT: *Imported beads: the outside necklace and four of the large beads in the center are examples of chevron beads, made in Venice since the 16th century and highly prized throughout Africa; the second necklace—of old and heavily worn beads—is from Mauritania and is made of amber, originally from the Baltic; the multi-colored tubular beads are glass millefiori imported from Venice; the red beads are from Amsterdam; only the large bluish white beads from southern Nigeria may be of local manufacture from recycled glass.*

Chapter Two

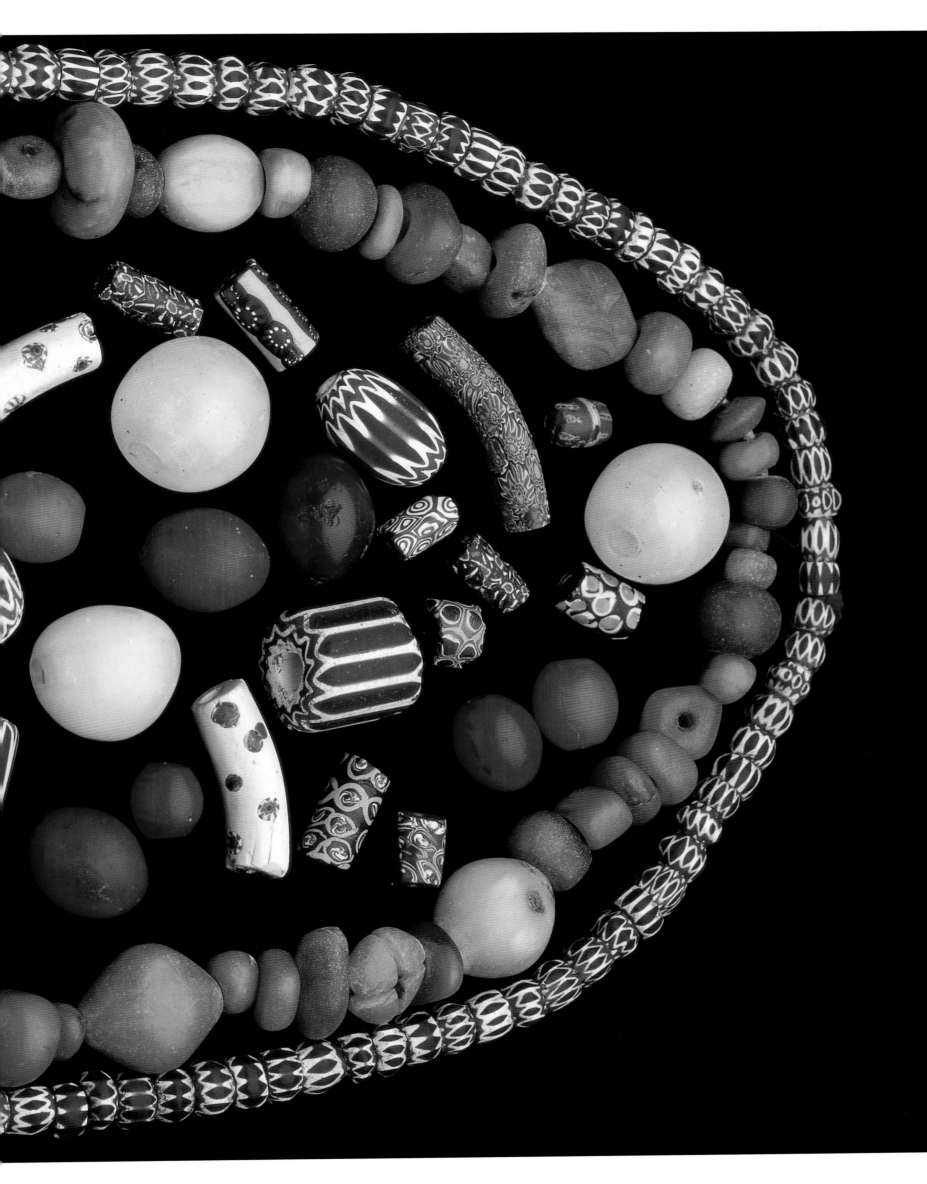

Bida, near the River Niger in central Nigeria. In the 1940s the anthropologist Nadel was able to witness the laborious three-day process which, even then, was being rapidly displaced by the melting down of European bottle glass. Today the glass beads of Bida, which are carried by Hausa traders over a wide expanse of West Africa, are entirely made from bottle glass. Colors made include brown, green, yellow, and blue, many with a white spiral added.

Glass beads are also quite widely manufactured from imported bottle glass in southern Ghana, with craftsmen of the Krobo people the acknowledged masters of the technique. Here the method used is somewhat different. The glass is ground down into a fine powder and poured into the holes of a prepared clay mold. A thin, green, leaf stem is pushed into the center of each bead to form the perforation. Stripes down the bead can be obtained by carefully forming a hole at the edge of the glass powder using another thin stem, then filling in the gap with powder of another color, while stripes across the bead were simply created by filling the space in the mold with layers of different colored powder. When the mold is fired it does not reach a sufficiently high temperature to melt the glass, instead it

ABOVE: Children of the Sango people, fishermen on the Ubangi river, with red and white beaded hairstyles. Another Central African Republic photograph taken in about, 1910.

RIGHT: Bracelets and beads from the Songhai region, Mali, laboriously carved from solid gneiss stone.

fuses the particles together forming a solid opaque bead.

The trade in imported beads into Africa is clearly an ancient one, although some more remote peoples did not gain ready access to beads in large quantities until the dawn of the colonial era late in the 19th century. Beads were carried into Africa by the caravans that have crossed the Sahara for several thousand years, and by the Arab coastal trade into East Africa, but moved onto a different, massive scale, with the development of glass bead-making technology in Venice and the Portuguese exploration of the African coastline in the 15th century. The main centers of glass bead production in Europe were Venice, Amsterdam, and, somewhat later, the town of Jablonec in today's Czech Republic. Factories in these towns became expert in catering for African tastes and preferences in terms of colors, sizes, and shapes of beads, often trying to

imitate locally manufactured beads. Sample cards were prepared and distributed so traders in Africa and travelers to the continent could select the most suitable types from the thousands available. Knowledge of what type of bead was popular in particular regions became vital for would-be explorers in the 19th century, since a miscalculation could leave them with heavy sacks of untradeable beads and no means of buying vital supplies. When stocking up in Zanzibar from the shiploads of beads imported from Europe, the explorer Henry Morten Stanley, writing in 1872, calculated he would need to take with him on his journey to Lake Tanganyika a total of 22 sacks of beads in 11 varieties. Among the most popular types were tiny glass seed beads in a huge range of colors, multi-colored Venetian *millefiore* (thousand flower), and the layered blue, red, and white chevron made in both Venice and Amsterdam since the 16th century.

Beadwork in West Africa varies from simple strands of waist beads to the beaded embroidery of the Yoruba and the bead-covered thrones and statues of the Cameroon grassfields region. Among the Yoruba of southwestern Nigeria, beaded clothing—and especially beaded crowns—are reserved for the ceremonial dress of kings. Conical crowns totally covered in an embroidery of tiny seed beads, with long fringes to cover the king's face, were made by specialist craftsmen working to royal order. Most of the bead artists were from one family—called Adeshina—from the small town of Efon-Alaye. They would travel to live as the guests of the local king while working on a new crown. The Yoruba trace their major kings back to descendants of Oduduwa, who, according to myth, climbed down from Heaven to found the world in the sacred city of Ife. Only kings able to make recognized claims to direct descent from Oduduwa are entitled to wear the beaded crowns. The head, *ori*, is the focus and embodiment of each king's sacred destiny and as such it is protected, concealed, and enhanced by the crown, which is itself a highly sacred and

RIGHT: *European glass trade beads popular in West Africa: Venetian millefiore (lower center) and chevron (upper center), multi-colored pear-shaped beads from Jablonec, Czech Republic.*

44

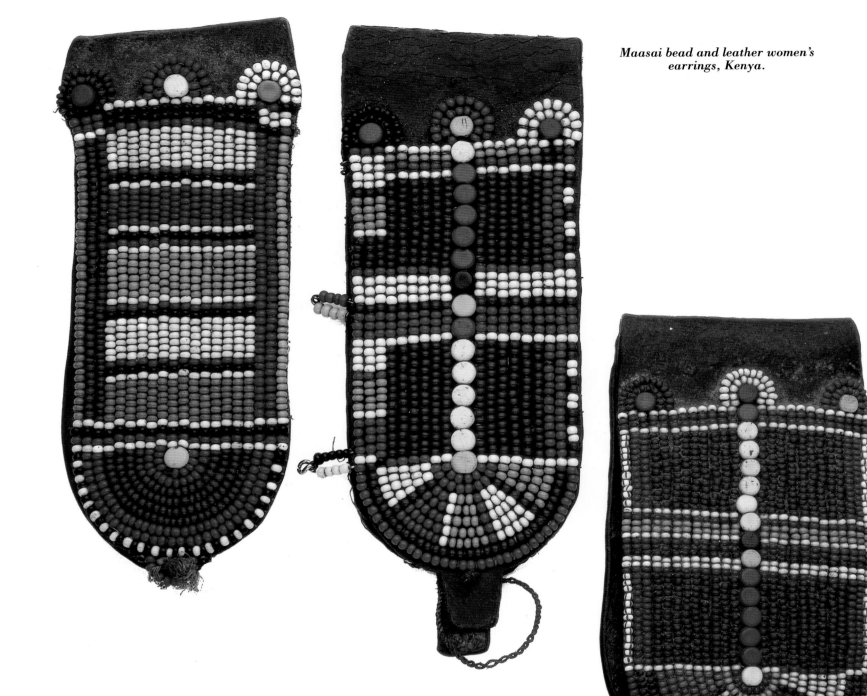

Maasai bead and leather women's earrings, Kenya.

ritually charged object. Other smaller crowns (without the beaded fringe) were made for use on less important occasions and by rulers not entitled to the full regalia. Yoruba kings also commissioned beadworkers to embroider robes, cushions, staffs, and other court items, while beaded bags were an important badge of office for *babalawo*, diviners who had mastered the secrets of the Ifa divination system.

Before the widespread adoption of Christianity or Islam in the 20th century, Yoruba religious practice involved a large number of deities, called *orisa*, who were subordinate to the supreme god, Olorun. Each orisa had a separate group of followers and priests who would be recognizable by the distinctive colors of their beaded necklaces and bracelets. Many of these color choices are still followed by devotees

of Yoruba-inspired religions in South and Central Americs, such as the Candomble of Brazil and Santeria of Cuba. Among the colored beads of major orisa are: red and white for Sango, god of thunder; maroon for his wife Oya, goddess of hurricanes; white for the creator orisa Orisala; black for the trickster deity Esu; and blue for the water goddess Yemoja.

On the other side of the African continent beads are a key element in the aesthetics of adornment that unites many of the cattle-keeping, pastoral peoples of Kenya, Tanzania, northern Uganda, and the southern reaches of Sudan and Ethiopia. Although the specifics vary from one group to another, these peoples, who

include the Maasai,
Turkana, Rendile, Gabra,
Samburu, and Pokot, have similar social systems by which both men
and women move during their life through a
number of clearly distinct stages. These different
phases, such as, in the case of male Maasai,
childhood, youth, warriorship, and elderhood,
are often separated by transitional phases or
rites of passage, which may be marked by such
features as changes in hairstyle and the temporary use of body painting. Beadwork throughout
this region is prepared by women and is a key
method of indicating a wide range of information
about personal status and the stage in the life
cycle an individual has attained. For example,
among the Maasai a particular type of long-bead-
ed earring may only be worn by women who have
sons that have attained warrior status. The
Samburu maintain that a woman should

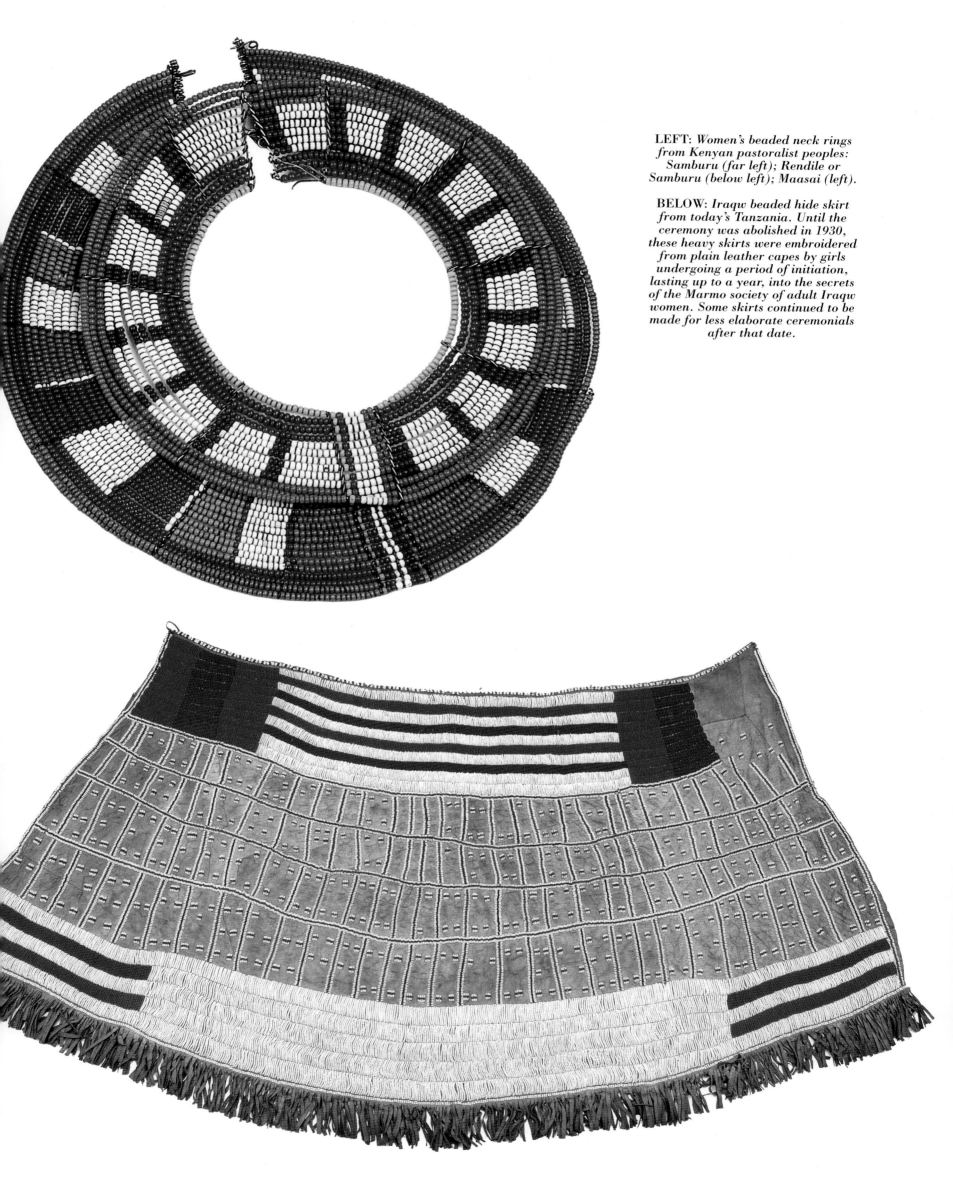

LEFT: *Women's beaded neck rings from Kenyan pastoralist peoples: Samburu (far left); Rendile or Samburu (below left); Maasai (left).*

BELOW: *Iraqw beaded hide skirt from today's Tanzania. Until the ceremony was abolished in 1930, these heavy skirts were embroidered from plain leather capes by girls undergoing a period of initiation, lasting up to a year, into the secrets of the Marmo society of adult Iraqw women. Some skirts continued to be made for less elaborate ceremonials after that date.*

accumulate sufficient beaded necklaces to support her chin completely, while Maasai women work their neck beads into distinctive flat discs. Beads form a woman's wealth, as cattle does a man's.

Although Europeans have long admired the color and variety of East African beadwork, it is only recently that some of the more complex nuances of local systems of aesthetics have begun to emerge from detailed research. In one of the most interesting papers, two American anthropologists, Donna Klumpp and Corinne Kratz, have explored the complexity of the similarities and differences between the beadwork of Maasai women and that of Okiek, who have lived in close proximity to the Maasai for centuries. They argue that, although women of the two groups have a broadly-shared understanding of the role of the dressed body, there are marked differences in the appreciation of the specifics of beadwork. In one example it is clear that a set of beads Okiek women admire because they feel it makes the wearer look both pretty and Maasai, fails to be appreciated by the Maasai themselves—both because they think it is only appropriate for the period on and after a woman's wedding, and because certain nuances of color arrangement in the beads have been changed. Although details of the colors used in Maasai beads change with fashion and availability, Maasai women maintain a complex system of balancing and breaking-up colors that, from their perspective, eludes attempts at imitation.

Many southern African peoples—such as the Transvaal Ndebele, Xhosa, and Zulu—are also well known for their beadwork. The Ndebele have become famous over the past few decades for their vibrant multi-colored wall-painting in a style that seems to have begun following their military defeat and forced dispersal as indentured laborers on white-owned farms in the 19th century. The emergence of a distinctive Ndebele style, reflected in both their women's mural designs and in beadwork and other items of women's dress, is closely connected both to the formation of a new sense of identity as a distinct people, and to their co-option by tourist promotion agencies keen to present an idealized image of tribal Africans

ABOVE: *Late 19th century photograph of a young Zulu woman, South Africa.*

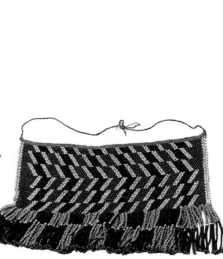

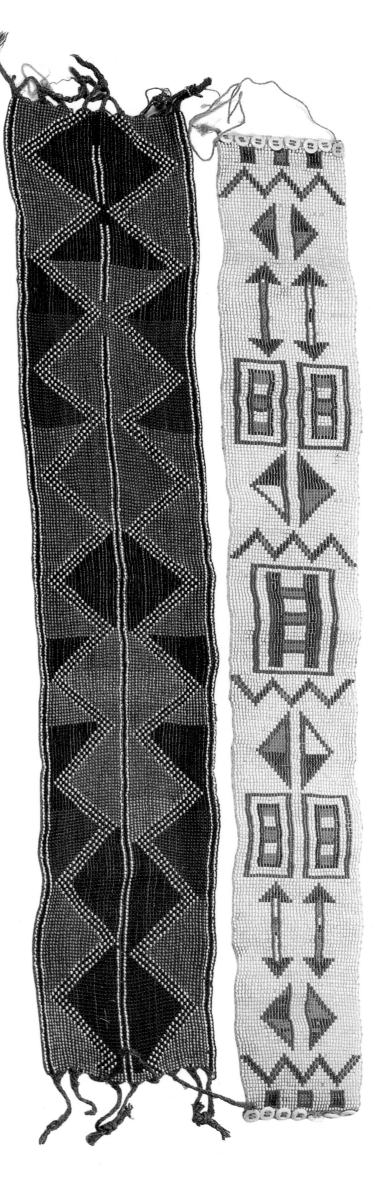

ABOVE: *Zulu beadwork girdles worn by young women over leather skirts, first half of 20th century.*

RIGHT: *Beaded sashes from Malawi (left) and the Kamba of Kenya (right).*

BELOW: *Hambukushu beaded apron from the Okavango region, Botswana. On reaching puberty a Hambukushu girl is presented with a beaded leather apron by her grandmothers, while other close female relatives contribute the beaded waistband and hanging panels shown here. Only when she has assembled the complete outfit to wear at the culmination of the puberty ceremonies can a young woman be properly initiated into adult status.*

under the apartheid government. Ndebele women wear a variety of beadwork-embroidered leather, and more recently plastic, garments such as aprons, together with beaded blankets, headbands, and bracelets. Many of these are indicative of a woman's marital status. Men wear beadwork on only a few occasions, mostly in connection with initiation into adulthood.

Both Xhosa and Zulu peoples living in rural areas of South Africa still produce and wear large quantities of beadwork, particularly on ceremonial occasions. These include collars, armbands, girls' aprons, bags, waistbands, and a variety of beaded clothing. There is a huge variety of regional variations in style and also marked changes in fashion over time. Although there may well be a long history of using locally-manufactured seed and shell beads in the region, the tiny glass beads from which most beadwork in the area is produced only became available in large quantities in the closing decades of the last century. Since

ABOVE: *Ndebele young woman's apron, South Africa.*

BELOW: *Zulu beadwork: men's sash/necklace, necklace, bag.*

RIGHT: *Zulu beaded neckbands worn by both men and women; Xhosa mens' collar.*

ABOVE: The two forms of beaded leather apron worn by Ndebele women to indicate their married status, lipotho (left) and ijogolo (right), mid-20th century.

TOP RIGHT: Ndebele married woman's apron, lipotho, early 20th century.

then beadwork traditions have emerged, flourished, and in many areas subsided again, despite the stimulus of the tourist industry. In the context of South Africa's troubled politics, dressing in a distinctively African or a distinctive ethnic style can take on a contemporary political significance. It is no coincidence that Nelson Mandela wore robes and a full set of Xhosa beadwork on the day he was sentenced to life imprisonment in 1962. More recently, the bloody rivalry between the African National Congress and the apartheid government-sponsored Zulu Inkatha party for control of the province of Kwa-Zulu Natal has prompted a self-conscious revival and promotion of Zulu cultural traditions in which the wide-scale wearing of beadwork on festive days has been a significant part.

One of the best-known aspects of South African beadwork is the so-called "Zulu love letter," a little panel of patterned beadwork on a necklace of beads which it was customary for a young girl to make as a present for her boyfriend. Recent scholars have been skeptical of the widely believed romantic theory that these gifts contained complicated color codes that could be translated by the young man into a message from his lover, with the suggestion that, for example blue and white striped beads symbolized striped locusts that cling together while mating and hence were a symbol of eternal love. Nevertheless it does seem to be the case that these gifts were part of a wider system of gift giving and symbolic communication in the process of courting, perhaps with more locally and contextually specific meanings.

DRESSING FOR CEREMONIAL AND EVERYDAY LIFE

Across the vast continent of Africa an extraordinarily rich variety of styles and traditions of dress have developed over many centuries, incorporating both local and imported materials. Although there are regions such as the Sahara desert in the north, the highlands of Ethiopia in the east, and Swaziland in the south, where extensive amounts of clothing are essential for protection against the extremes of the weather, in most areas clothing is a social rather than a physiological necessity. Indeed, the minimum requirement to be appropriately dressed varied with local ideas of modesty and decorum, and in rare cases—such as the cattle-keeping Nuer and Dinka of southern Sudan—could at times be as little as a string of waist beads; however, only those who were somehow not fully members of society, such as the insane, could disregard these conventions. Clothing is an important medium through which social status may be constructed and displayed. In both everyday and ceremonial attire, different societies in Africa developed often complex and

ABOVE: *A senior elder of the Ngongo group of the Kuba people, Kasai region, Congo, circa 1920. He wears an embroidered raffia skirt, beaded headband, cowrie shell-covered hat, anklets and bracelet.*

RIGHT: *A Kuba man's dancing skirt of raffia, Kasai region, Congo.*

sophisticated systems through which local ideas about authority, gender, age, seniority, and wealth were expressed. Contrary to the older impression of African clothing styles as invariably static, as scholars begin to research the history of dress in the different regions of Africa, it is becoming apparent that, within the framework of many of these local traditions, there was room for frequent innovation and changes in fashion.

Knowledge of the history of clothing in Africa still remains somewhat limited. Archaeological research in areas of Africa (apart from Egypt) has been relatively sporadic, and the climatic and soil conditions are mostly unfavorable to the preservation of textiles. For sub-Saharan Africa, written evidence is available only from isolated remarks in the second-hand accounts of a few scholars, such as Herodotus in European antiquity, from the chronicles of Arab travelers over the last millennium, and from European visitors since the 15th century exploration of the African coastline. Although numerous fragments of ancient textiles are known from Egypt, the

ABOVE: A 1930s view of King N'jiké of Banganté, Cameroons, with indigo resist-dyed skirt, ivory bracelets, necklaces, and beaded pipe.

RIGHT AND FAR RIGHT (DETAIL): A court official of the Asantehene of Kumasi, wearing a cloth hand-printed in the nearby village of Ntonso with adinkra designs. Ghana, 1997.

picture for sub-Saharan Africa is far less clear.

Spindle whorls and other evidence of weaving have been found at Meroë in the Sudan. Among the oldest textiles known are a red, green, and blue tunic and a shawl, both with what appear to be small figures embroidered on them, recently excavated from a burial site in the Republic of Niger. These cloths, which have been dated to the second half of the 8th century, are from a region criss-crossed by long distance trade routes and are perhaps a pointer to the importance of trade in the later history of African weaving. Small fragments of woven bast fiber dated to the 9th century were found at Igbo Ukwu in southeastern Nigeria. Large quantities of clothing fragments—which would seem to include both locally woven and imported cloths dating back to around the 11th century—have been recovered from burial sites in caves along the Bandiagara cliffs in Mali. That clothing was used as a marker of rank is apparent in one of the earliest accounts we have of an African court. Writing in the 11th century, the Arab traveler al-Bakri noted that at the court of the ancient empire of Ghana (which ruled large areas of present day Mali and Mauretania from around the 6th century) only the king and his heir were permitted to wear tailored garments, while the other nobles were restricted to loose robes of cotton or (imported) silk.

The raw materials used in the production of clothing in Africa include animal skins, bast fibers, wool, cotton, silk, raffia, and tree bark. The skins of both wild and domesticated animals were used for clothing throughout most of the African continent, although the increasing availability of imported cloth and the declining numbers of large game animals over the last century or so has made this practice far less widespread. There were large areas of eastern and southern Africa where weaving was not known and animal skins provided the main source of clothing.

LEFT: *Yoruba elder in agbada robe of hand-embroidered locally woven aso oke cloth, Ibadan, Nigeria, 1960s. His cap is made from a fashionable imported damask.*

RIGHT: *A Yoruba woman dressed in locally woven cotton and lurex aso oke cloth to celebrate the naming of her new baby. Oyo, Nigeria, 1996.*

Bast fibers—produced by allowing the stalks of plants such as jute or flax to decompose in water for a few days—would seem to have been far more widely woven in the past than it has in the 20th century. Linen woven from bast fibers was the material used in the weaving of ancient Egypt, source of some of the oldest surviving garments in the world. Wool is the major fiber used to make both clothing and tent cloths by the women weavers of the Berber peoples of North Africa, as well as by men of Arab origin weaving in the urban workshops of the region. Elsewhere in Africa weaving with animal fibers is quite rare, since most types of sheep in sub-Saharan Africa do not produce wool. Weaving with sheep's wool is found only among the Fulani weavers of the inland Niger delta in Mali, in parts of Sudan, and in southern Madagascar.

Cotton has been cultivated across a wide expanse of the Sahel and savanna regions of Africa for more than a thousand years, with some of the earliest evidence for cotton textiles coming from 5th century sites of the kingdom of Meroë in present day Sudan, and for much of the present millennium cotton cloth has been woven from Senegal to Nigeria, across the continent to Ethiopia.

Silk is not a widely used fiber in African weaving but in areas where it was used it often took on considerable significance; for instance the import of silk into West Africa has a long history. Since the 17th century imported silk cloths were unraveled by Asante weavers in Ghana to provide the colors needed to develop kente for the Asante court. In the 19th century large quantities of magenta-colored waste silk from the textile factories of France and Italy was shipped across the Mediterranean to Tripoli, from where it was carried on the long journey by camel across the Sahara to Kano in northern Nigeria. Much of it ended up hundreds of miles further south where together with cotton and sanyan, a local wild silk, it was used by Yoruba and Nupe weavers to weave the large flowing robes popularized by the ruling Fulani aristocracy following the Islamic jihad which swept across northern Nigeria at the beginning of the 19th century. These robes, often with complex silk or cotton embroidery by Nupe, Yoruba, or Hausa specialists, became the predominant dress of kings, chiefs, and wealthy men across a large swathe of West Africa. In the 20th century the importation of European waste silk ended with the decline of the trans-Saharan trade, and imported silks have been supplanted by rayon and other synthetic fibers.

Raffia is produced from the younger leaves of several species of palm tree that grow throughout most of the forested regions of sub-Saharan Africa. Lengths of about five or six foot of fiber can be sliced from the thin upper skin of the developing leaves, dried in the sun, then split lengthways with a comb or fingernails to produce narrow pliable fibers that can be woven into a quite soft and flexible cloth. In this century it has continued to be woven in parts of West Africa, such as among the southern Igbo, throughout the Zaire basin, and also in Madagascar although there primarily for use as ceremonial dress and at funerals.

Bark cloth is felted, a bit like paper, rather woven. Bark is stripped in a single piece from the trunk of a suitable tree, moistened with water or steam, and then carefully hammered with a special beater. This is a highly skilled task during which the cloth may be expanded by up to four or five times, producing a thin but even and quite strong fabric. The best known regions for bark cloth production are Zaire, Uganda, Rwanda, and Malawi, but it is known that the Asante of Ghana used to manufacture bark cloth which still has some ritual uses.

Scholars mostly now accept that although some of the loom types found in Africa—such as the pit loom used in Ethiopia—are clearly of external origin, the fundamental technology used to weave cloth for use as clothing was probably independently developed. Although a wide variety of different looms are used in Africa, they may be divided into two categories based on a key difference in the way in which the warp threads (those threads that are held in tension by the loom) are manipulated. The set of warp threads has to be divided into two groups to allow the crosswise threads (the weft) to be interlaced across them in a regular fashion. When this is achieved by attaching a rod (called a heddle) by loops to one of the groups of warp threads, the loom is called single-heddle, while looms where the other group of warps is also leashed to a second heddle are known as double-heddle.

The single-heddle looms found in Africa include the ground loom used for weaving tent cloths by Berber women, a second type of vertically mounted Berber loom, the vertical loom used mostly by women in Nigeria, various types of vertical raffia looms used from eastern Nigeria into Zaire, and various simple ground looms used along the Nigeria–Cameroon border and formerly in large areas of East Africa. The most important double-heddle loom is the West African treadle loom, whose distinguishing features include the use of a weighted dragsled to

tension the warp. On this type of loom cloth is usually woven in long, thin strips, sometimes as narrow as an inch, but more commonly about four to six inches, which are then sewn together edge-to-edge to make the completed cloth. The eastern reach of this loom around Lake Chad almost meets the western limits of a type of double-heddle pit loom used by the weavers of Ethiopia. Others looms include the Mende tripod loom and a variety of obscure variants of the treadle loom in Sierra Leone, together with the looms introduced by Arabs to North Africa, and by Europeans in the colonial period.

Although large quantities of plain white cloth were woven, much of the cloth used for clothing in Africa was decorated, either during the process of weaving, or subsequently. The complexities of decorative weaving are too numerous and diverse to discuss here, but in summary, African weavers utilize a limited set of

RIGHT: *Cotton and imported silk robe of the type first woven and embroidered mostly by Nupe craftsmen for the courts of the Fulani aristocracy of the Sokoto Caliphate, northern Nigeria. Subsequently they became the favored dress of senior men throughout Nigeria.*

BELOW: *Design on the back of a Yoruba man's robe woven and embroidered with local hand-spun wild silk known as sanyan, circa 1950.*

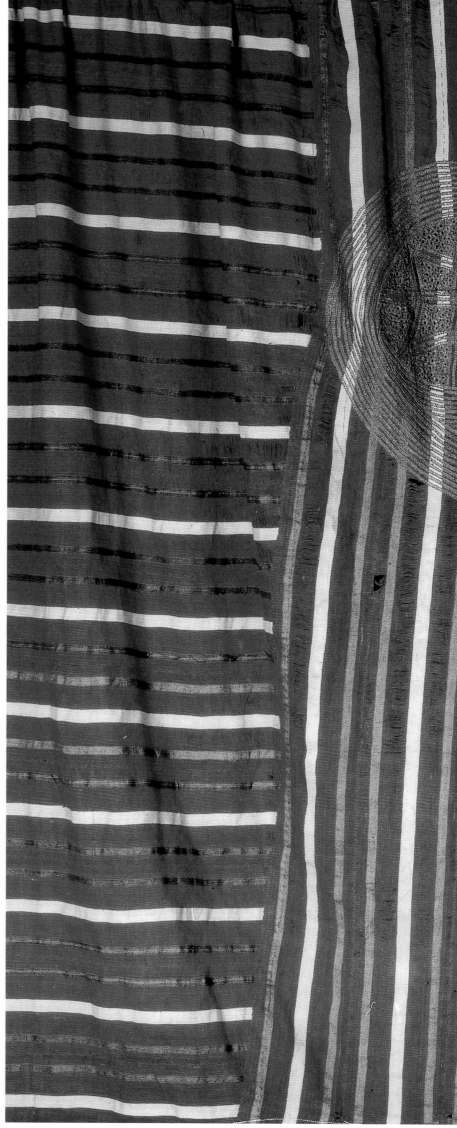

techniques that includes float weaving, where extra threads float across (or more rarely down) a piece of cloth, openwork, tapestry weave, pile weave, and weft inserts.

The main method of decorating cloth throughout Africa is the dyeing of thread or completed cloths. A range of locally-produced plant dyes allowed weavers in most areas to produce a few shades of brown, green, yellow, and in some cases red, but by far the most important dye in Africa has been indigo. The vast majority of cloth produced on the continent over the centuries was simple designs produced by combining the natural white of the cotton fibers with stripes of various shades of indigo blue. Dyeing was itself an important business at which high degrees of specialist skill was developed in centers such as the Hausa city of Kano. Very thin, fine quality, narrow-strip cloth dyed a dark indigo in the village of Kura near Kano, then carefully beaten with extra indigo paste by specialist cloth beaters until it took on a glazed sheen, are still an extremely expensive and highly valued cloth, worn as face veils by Tuareg and other nomads throughout North Africa.

Dyers have also utilized a variety of methods of resist dyeing, i.e. the dyeing of thread or fabric which has been treated so that part of it resists the dye, leaving a pattern on the cloth. These include ikat weaving among the Baule of Côte D'Ivoire and the Yoruba of Nigeria and a number of traditions that utilize starch-resist or tie and dye, of which the adire of the Yoruba is best known. Various types of brightly-colored resist-dyeing using imported cloth and industrially produced dyes are now extremely widespread in countries such as Nigeria, Mali, Sierra Leone, and Senegal. In the village of Ntonso near the Asante capital of Kumase specialist workers still utilize a type of printing using stamps made from sections of calabash shell to produce a patterned cloth called adinkra, that is widely worn in southern Ghana, especially for funerals and at courts. Embroidery is found in numerous styles, including on the raffia cloths of Zaire and the robes of northern Nigeria.

Utilizing some of these techniques textile workers in Africa have developed a wide variety of local styles and traditions which have contributed to the development of notions of localized group identity, as people of a particular area often dressed in a distinctive cloth design or clothing style allowing them to be readily distinguished from strangers and travelers. This assisted in the formation of senses of tribal or ethnic identity in the colonial period, with textile forms among the cultural resources available for the construction of new dimensions of group identity. A conventionalized picture of "tribal" dress styles, for example, for the Yoruba, Igbo, and Hausa of Nigeria, often developed, although usually from a considerable oversimplification of the true complexity of local textile fashions. The existence of these localized styles in the pre-colonial period was also the basis for much of the long-distance trade in textiles. Cloth did not just move from weaving areas to clothe people in regions where no cloth was produced. Equally, if not more important, was the demand for different types of cloth than could be produced in the home region. Kings, chiefs, and wealthy traders sought to enhance their prestige by accumulating and displaying the sheer variety of cloths accessible to them. In many regions these included numerous European and Asian fabrics imported into Africa for centuries, which competed with, but in most areas did not displace, local textile production.

It is often wrongly asserted by commentators that fashion is an attribute only of the Western capitalist system to be contrasted, favorably or otherwise, with the supposed stability of dress styles in so-called "traditional societies." In fact the evidence would seem to suggest that at least some aspects of dress are subject to the vagaries of fashion in virtually all societies. As far as Africa is concerned, in the 17th century, European merchants on the Gold Coast were complaining that the annual changes in local taste for imported cloth was leaving them with cargoes of unsaleable merchandise to return to Europe. Although in some cases the popular designs of local weavers changed little over many years, in others, such as the aso oke cloth worn by the Yoruba, weavers were continually experimenting with novel designs. In the 20th century, and particularly in the years since the 1960s when many African nations recovered their inde-

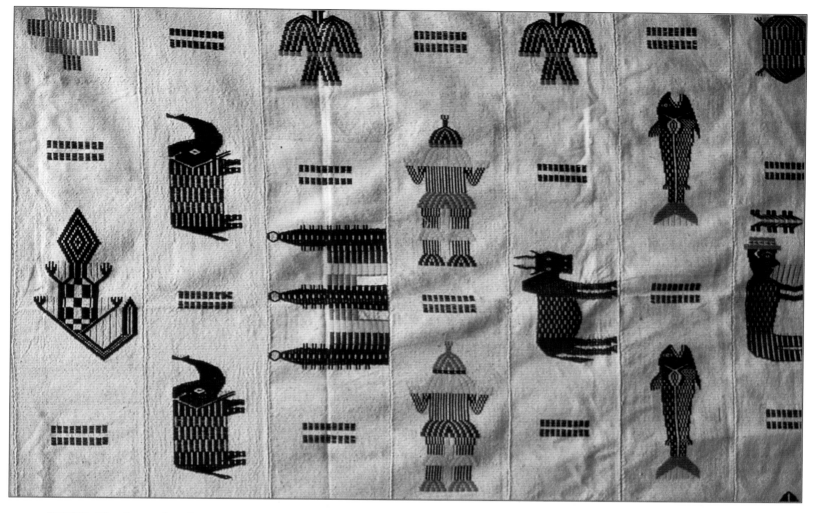

ABOVE: Hand spun local cotton cloth from Bobo Dioulasso, Burkina Faso, with weft float motifs depicting a farmer at work, a masquerader, a mosque, and various animals.

BELOW: An Asante weaver at Bonwire, the royal weaving village, carefully adds decorative weft motifs by hand to the narrow strip of cloth, Ghana, 1997.

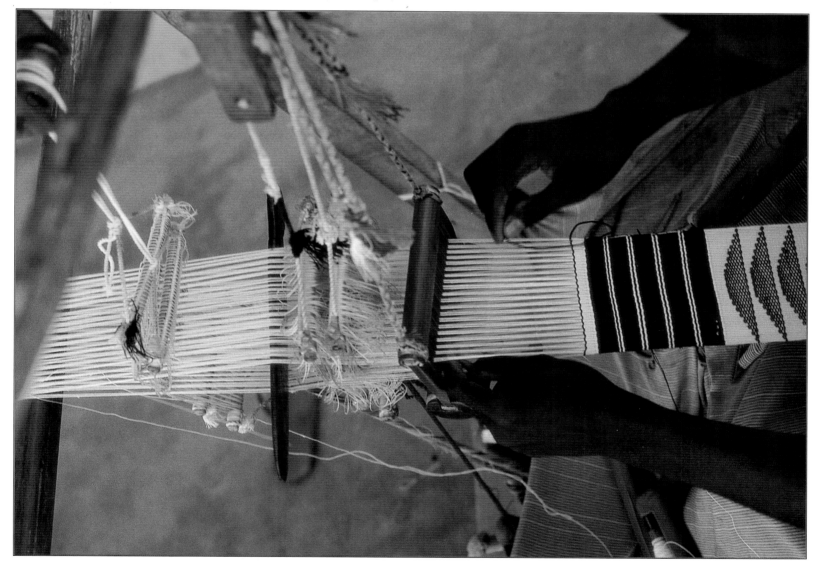

pendence, the extent of African contacts with Europe and America have dramatically increased. The wide availability in urban communities over recent decades of magazines, then television, video, and most recently satellite television, coupled with easy access for the wealthy to Europe and the USA, has transformed the range of references from which local fashions are drawn. Styles propagated by the wealthy are quickly copied and dispersed among students and urban workers. In some cases these fashions are entirely based around local responses to imported clothing, as in the notorious "Sapeurs," an informal association of self-proclaimed fashion victims of Kinshasa lead by the Zairean music star Papa Wemba. More usually though, there is an influence from, and an incorporation of, international fashions into aspects of local dress.

The impact of these developments on African dress goes beyond the selective adoption of new materials such as synthetic fibers and lurex. Many designers working in Africa are attempting to give their work a local appeal by using regional traditions of weaving and textile design in contemporary dress styles. This

ABOVE: An Asante male wrapper cloth, from 20th century Ghana, with characteristic alternating sections of warp and weft-faced plain weave and supplementary weft float decoration.

RIGHT: An Asante woman's silk wrapper cloth, Ghana, 20th century.

is particularly apparent with a growing number of designers active in the 1990s working between Paris and the capitals of Francophone Africa from Dakar and Abidjan to Niamey, including the late Chris Seydou, Xuly Bët, and Alphadi.

Two African dress styles, kente and bogolanfini, in particular have become the focus of worldwide interest with reproductions of the fabrics now manufactured in countries from the United States to India. Kente is the name now given to the brightly colored narrow-strip cloth, originally woven from silk, but more recently primarily of cotton and rayon, that was the court dress of

the Asante empire. The wealth of the Asante empire was based on control over the gold mining districts of present-day Ghana, allowing the Asantehene and lesser rulers to maintain courts which, as we saw in the account quoted in the Introduction, were of unprecedented splendor. Some silk cloth designs were reserved for the sole use of the king himself, while he granted rights to wear other designs to favored allies and court officials. As is still the case today, the finest cloths were woven in Bonwire, a village of specialized craftsmen near the capital. The cloth was never tailored into garments. Instead men would wear a single large cloth draped around their body, leaving one shoulder bare in toga fashion, while women wore two rather smaller cloths. Usually the first formed a wrapper, covering the body from the breasts to the knees, while the second was folded as a shawl and draped over one shoulder. Alternatively women could tie both cloths as wrappers, one around the waist, the other under the arms. The present worldwide popularity of kente stems from the late 1950s when the first president of independent Ghana, Kwame Nkrumah, a leading figure in the Pan-Africanist movement, began to wear it to international gatherings.

Bogolanfini, a type of mud-dyed cloth from the region of Mali inhabited by Bamana peoples has become internationally known far more recently, mostly as a result of its use as an inspiration for fashion by local designers such as Chris Seydou, and its adoption by well known African musicians during the "world music" boom of the late 1980s. It too has subsequently become a popular feature of Afrocentric dress in the Americas. Although much of the bogolan for export is made using stencils by male students in the Malian capital Bamako, in its home regions

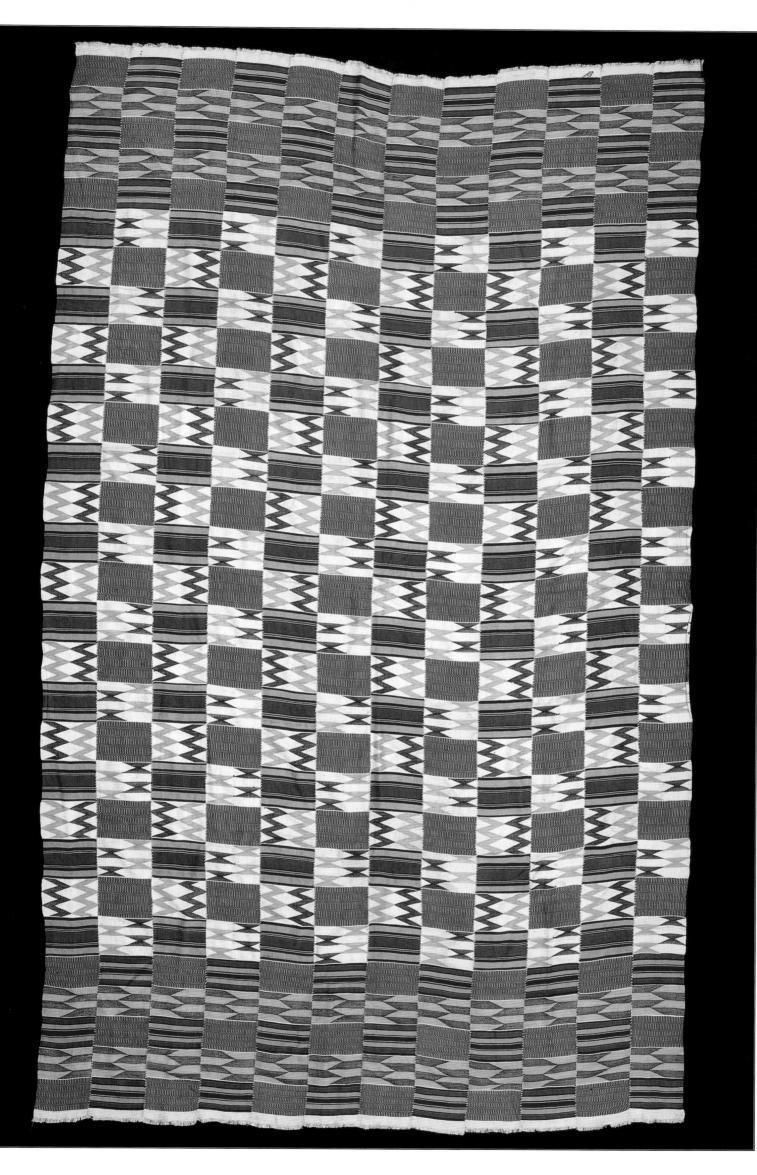

*An unusually elaborate example of an Ewe male wrapper cloth
with figurative supplementary weft float decoration; from the
Volta region of Ghana, 20th century.*

the cloth is hand painted by local women. Using a unique and complex process which involves several different applications of dyes made from iron-rich mud and plant extracts, the women outline the designs in black, leaving a negative unpainted pattern area. Many of the individual patterns have names, such as the cross shape set diagonally within a square, which is called "Mauretanian woman's head-cushion" after the expensive embroidered leather cushions such women own and has implications of both femininity and wealth. Scholarly opinion differs however over whether the entire design on locally used cloth can be decoded to provide some kind of meaning. Certain types of bogolanfini were, and in some areas still are, mainly worn by young women undergoing initiation into adulthood, a process involving the ritually and physically dangerous procedures of circumcision. Bogolanfini was also used in the dress of men such as hunters, and more recently, musicians. Today the cloth has become virtually a national symbol in Mali and is tailored into garments such as jackets, hats, and waistcoats for local as well as export use.

LEFT: Ethiopian dress hand-woven of cotton and silk, worn with a matching shawl for church services.

ABOVE: Mud-resist dyed bogolanfini cloth, worn by hunters and by young girls undergoing initiation into womanhood among the Bamana people of Mali.

RIGHT: Plaited raffia fibre women's buttock ornament (egbe) worn for dances, northeastern Congo, early 20th century.

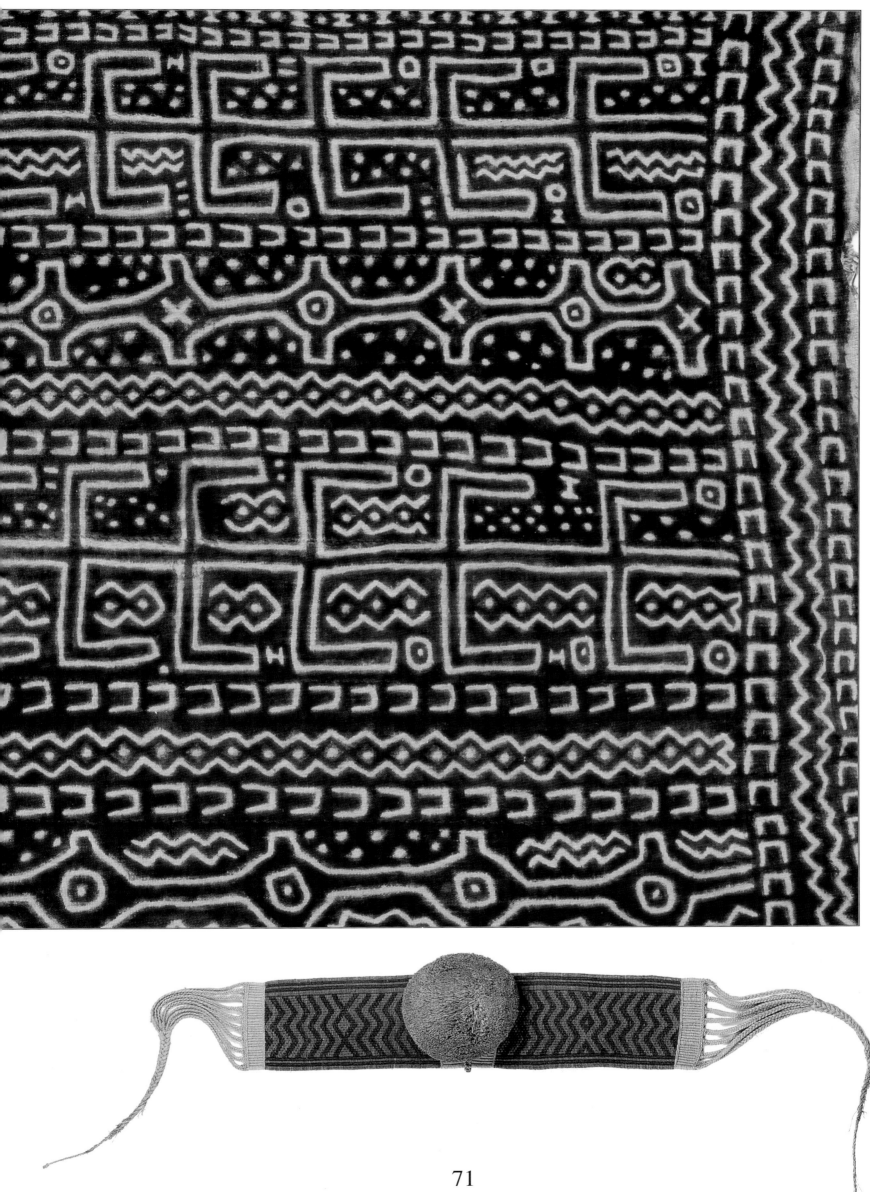

DISPLAYING THE HEAD

AFRICAN HATS AND HEADDRESSES

In 1909 a missionary visiting the Cameroon grassfields kingdom of Bamun observed its ruler, Sultan Njoya, participating in a ceremonial dance wearing a crown so large and heavy that as he danced it had to be held in place by a servant hiding behind him. Men of the Karomojong of Kenya and Uganda use mud and ochre to fashion their hair into a solid, brightly-painted headdress set with clusters of ostrich feathers. When they get bored with the design, it can be cut off in one piece and, in recent years, sold to an art gallery.

Elaborate and ornate hairstyles have long been a vital component of correct dress in numerous African societies, combining individual creativity with the reproduction of familiar local styles to display key aspects of social identity. Paralleling the attention given to creating both beautiful and meaningful hairstyles has been the development of an amazing variety of hats and headdresses. Although hats are often overlooked in the study of African art the range of formal variation achieved through the manipulation of both local and imported materials is truly extraordinary. Equally significant is their important role alongside other dimensions of dress and adornment in both daily life and the marking of ceremonial occasions.

In many societies in Africa it is regarded as correct adult dress to cover the head when in public. Even those hats that fulfil this basic social need, as with others that protect the wearer from the hazards of sun or rain, are frequently the products of great skill, achieving balanced compositions in readily available materials such as cloth and raffia. More exotic materials, precious metals, rare bird feathers, or animal skins are often the insignia of the hats and crowns of chiefs and kings. Hats can indicate occupational status, as do those covered in amulets and the relics of wild beasts displayed by men in many West African communities who follow the dangerous trade of a hunter. They can indicate a woman's marital status to potential admirers. They can, as do the veils worn by Tuareg men in the Sahara, protect the wearer from the dangerous and polluting effects of interacting with others. As with the doffing of hats in European greetings in the past, covering or uncovering the head is used to indicate different levels of respect or superiority.

ABOVE: Mangbetu elder with feather-decorated plaited fiber hat, northeastern Congo, circa 1910.

RIGHT: Mossi dancer's hat, made from a calabash covered with plaited leather, with horn, animal hair, and cowrie shell attachments. Worn at dances held for the funeral of elders, Burkina Faso, 20th century.

Underlying this diversity of forms and uses are a number of widely shared ideas about the importance of the head as the seat of individual identity, intelligence, and personal destiny. We will briefly consider two examples from widely different societies: the desert dwelling Tuareg and the urban Yoruba. The Tuareg are a semi-nomadic people found in a vast area of southern Libya and northern Mali and Niger. One of the names by which the Tuareg refer to themselves is "People of the Veil." Unlike other Muslim societies, however, it is adult men not women who must cover their head and face with long flowing veils of gauzy indigo or white cloth. This requirement is attributed not to Islamic doctrine, but to earlier Tuareg notions of the significance of the head. According to the anthropologist Susan Rasmussen, for the Tuareg the head serves as the seat of intelligence, but all of its orifices are both sources of pollution to others and vulnerable points through which a person may be afflicted with misfortune. For men in particular it is important to veil the face both as a sign of respect to others and to cover up potential points of access from the dangers posed by such threats as gossip and the evil eye. The position of the veil may be altered depending on whether a man is in the presence of his seniors or his wife's relatives, or simply with junior men or strangers. For women, especially married women, it is important to cover the hair with a headscarf as a sign of modesty, but concealing the face is not usually considered necessary.

ABOVE: *A Zulu sangoma, a professional healer, diviner and spirit medium, using chalk, feathers, and an assemblage of products of the wild to distinguish herself from normal attire.*

LEFT: *Fang detachable hairpiece/hats from Gabon, 20th century. These hats were worn for everyday use by ordinary people, with some designs shared by both men and women, while others are reserved for just one sex.*

The Yoruba are town-dwelling people of the forest and savanna regions of southwestern Nigeria, pursuing farming, trading, and a huge range of modern occupations from university professors to bus drivers. Despite the spread of Christianity and Islam in the 20th century, older ideas about the importance of the head are still widely shared. The Yoruba word for head, *ori*, refers not just to the outwardly visible head, but to the much more important inner head, the seat of personal destiny. Good fortune is described as *ori ire*, literally "good head." According to Yoruba myth, each individual before his or her birth has the opportunity to kneel before God and choose from a selection of heads available their own head, which represents their destiny in life. Unfortunately it is not possible to tell before choosing the head whether the selected destiny will be good or bad, and once born the child forgets what has been chosen. It was then necessary to make repeated trips to a diviner to consult the deity Orunmila, who knows each person's destiny, in order to make sure that the correct path was followed. Important men would make leather shrines dedicated to their heads, which were covered with cowrie shells (used as money) in a visible representation of good fortune. The head is also the seat of *ase*, the mystic power to make things happen, to energize the universe so that one's words came to pass.

The ultimate expression of the Yoruba reverence for the head was the beaded royal crown

LEFT: *Chief of one of the peoples of the Unyoro kingdom in present day Uganda. His extraordinary hat combines feathers, animal fibers, shells, and dried plants in a complex construction which a contemporary source noted, required constant attention to maintain.*

ABOVE: *Married Herero women from Namibia or Botswana, their three-pointed leather headdress, called ekori, seems to have been linked to the horns of the cattle on which their wealth was based. Photograph dated to the late 19th century.*

RIGHT: *Yoruba women are known for the wide range of ways in which they can wrap the cloth of their gele or headtie, with fashionable variations spreading rapidly. This photograph from Ibadan, Nigeria, 1996.*

(see the illustrations in Chapter 2). These conical crowns, totally covered with bead designs, concealed within them relics which served to enhance the mystic power of the king's head, a process also achieved by inserting certain substances into cuts in the crown of his head during the coronation rituals. In addition to different examples of the veiled conical crown that confirmed his claim to descent from the founding deity of Yoruba kings, many rulers would also have several smaller beaded crowns for less ritually important occasions. Perhaps the most interesting of these were the playful white-beaded replicas of English barristers' wigs that some kings adopted in the first half of this century for use while sitting in judgement in the local courts established under the colonial system of Indirect Rule.

For ordinary Yoruba men and women the main head coverings are the men's cap or *fila*, and the women's headtie or *gele*. Few adults will be seen in public without them, and they are certainly essential for any formal occasion. One style of cap that was popular for many years was embroidered with brass or silver wire on a velvet base. The cost of such a cap was high—up to 12 shillings in the 1940s if silver was used. An account from the 19th century reports that Basorun Samoye of Abeokuta—one of a new style of wealthy leaders that flourished in a period of continuous warfare—wore a cap embroidered with gold, while in Lagos up to the 1840s only the king could wear this type of hat. Fashions in both caps and headties change frequently, and there is great scope for individual inventiveness in improvising new variations on familiar forms. This is particularly true of women's headties, where the basic garment of a large rectangular piece of cloth may be wrapped and tied in an almost infinite variety of ways. An

LEFT: *Mende chief in war costume, Sierra Leone, late 19th century. Both his hat and his robe are sewn with packages containing amulets to protect him in battle. Around his neck he wears another amulet in a silver case.*

ABOVE: *Feathers were used to make distinctive hats for prominent individuals across a wide area of Africa. This posed studio photograph from late 19th century Natal depicts a Swazi warrior in ceremonial regalia.*

RIGHT: *A Yoruba oba or king wearing his beaded crown, Nigeria, 1960s. Yoruba kings are believed to have divine status and the veil of beads, which was always worn in public until recent years, served to protect his subjects from the potential danger of seeing his uncovered face.*

elegantly-shaped and flamboyant headtie will be much admired and commented on at any public gathering. Both locally woven and imported cloths are used for gele, with the most expensive and fashionable styles being made for the Nigerian market by specialist companies in Switzerland.

Cloth, beads, and precious metals may be used in the making of African hats, demonstrating publicly the wealth and status of the wearer. Other materials that are particularly important in many communities are those drawn from the wild, from the bush or forest. Associated with the dangerous powers of domains outside the cultivated order of the village, they are particularly appropriate for the hats and caps of chiefs, hunters, diviners, and others whose role brings them into contact with the animals and spirits of the wilderness. Many hats utilize feathers both as rare objects of beauty and for their symbolic allusions to the wealth of different qualities associated different bird species. The huge feather

headdresses worn by chiefs, prominent officials, and important dancers at celebrations among the Tikar and neighboring Cameroon peoples are perhaps the most spectacular of a vast range of African feathered hats. The bright orange or pink feathers are skillfully sewn onto a raffia fiber base in such a way that they splay out widely in use, but can be neatly folded inside-out for storage in between festivities.

Like feathers, the skins and fur of animals are often selected as much for their symbolic resonances as for their dramatic appearance. Colobus monkey fur, leopard skin, snake skin, and even the bones and skulls of small animals were frequently used. Leopards are a recurrent symbol of chieftaincy and kingship, while monkeys are often associated with divination. The scale-like skin of the pangolin—a small mammal that rolls into an impenetrable ball when attacked—is a widely reported symbolic material, drawing on the animal's ability to resist the fiercest predators. Hunters' and warriors' caps

are often bedecked with animal horns, which both indicate their prowess and serve as containers for amulets and protective medicines. A remarkable horned hat utilizing the spiky skin of the blowfish was used in youths' initiation rites by the Bidjogo of Guinea Bissau.

In some cases hats may indicate membership of a society or the wearer's rank within it. In his discussion of the Bwami society, a highly complex organization by which the wealth and authority of elders was channeled to benefit the community among the Lega people of the Congo (formerly Zaire), art historian Daniel Biebuyck has reported that, while a large range of hats made of raffia ornamented with beads, buttons, and cowries, are insignia of men's and women's rank, other types—including hats made from

such wild materials as pangolin skin, iguana skin, the ear of an elephant, or the skin of the forest crocodile—are the individual fancy and improvisation of prominent elders.

One source of inspiration for hat designs was the replication of hairstyles. Since many of the more elaborate hairstyles often involved the incorporation of extra hair, plant fibers, mud, feathers, and numerous other items, the distinction between detachable versions of these styles as wigs, and hats of similar design becomes blurred. The Pende are a matrilineal people living to the west of the Kasai river in the recently renamed Congo. One distinctive Pende hairstyle, once worn by both men and women, involved using red earth to shape the hair into a long central crest, wide at the nape of the neck,

ABOVE: *Beaded chief's hat, misango mayaka, adopted by Yaka chiefs from the neighboring Pende in the first decades of the 20th century. The horns are thought to allude to the strength of the buffalo.*

RIGHT: *A 20th century chief's hat, mpu a nzim, of the Mbala, southwestern Congo.*

narrowing to a curled under point at the fore-
head. The hairline and the edges of the crest
were decorated with copper nails, beads, or
cowrie shells. An identical hairstyle could be
constructed from black fiber, also decorated
with copper studs or shells, allowing it to be
worn as a detachable wig or hat called a
mukotte. Reports indicate that although the style
was dying out in the early decades of this century its popularity increased at the time of a revolt
against the Belgian colonial regime in the
mid-1930s.

Each type of African hat has its own complex
history, representing diverse aspects of the social
structure, history, material resources and
aesthetic preferences of the people who made
and wore it. It is only in the last few years that
scholars have begun to look to museum collections and archives of old photographs to recog-

*ABOVE LEFT AND ABOVE: Early 20th century photographs
showing Fang women from Gabon wearing fiber, cowrie shells,
brass studs, buttons, and beads in their hair. In some cases these
were detachable, others were woven together with the hair.*

*RIGHT: Fang detachable hairpiece/hats from Gabon, 20th
century. These hats were worn for everyday use by ordinary
people, with some designs shared by both men and women,
while others were reserved for a single sex.*

nize some of the creativity revealed in these elaborate and often extravagant forms. Meanwhile people within Africa continue to adapt, adopt, improvise and innovate, discarding some older styles but evolving new and novel ones, drawing on an ever wider range of sources.

LEFT: *Yoruba royal beaded crown in the form of a judge's wig from Nigeria, 20th century. Under the British colonial system of Indirect Rule, Yoruba kings sat as judges in local courts. Some of them commissioned these crowns from their beadworkers in a witty imitation of the English judicial wigs they saw in the higher courts of the capital.*

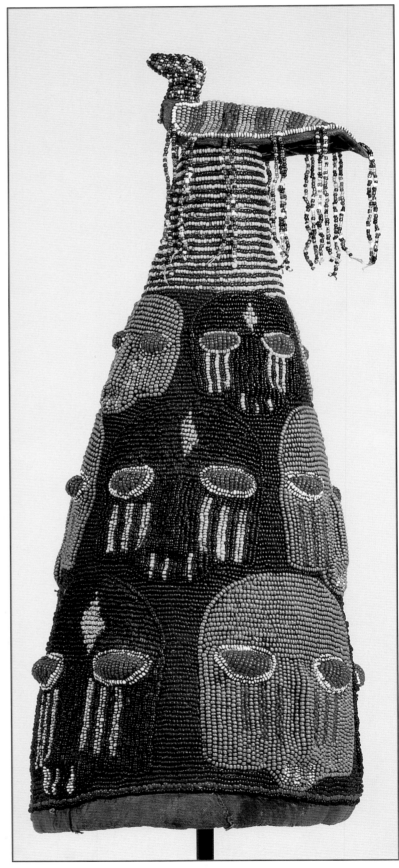

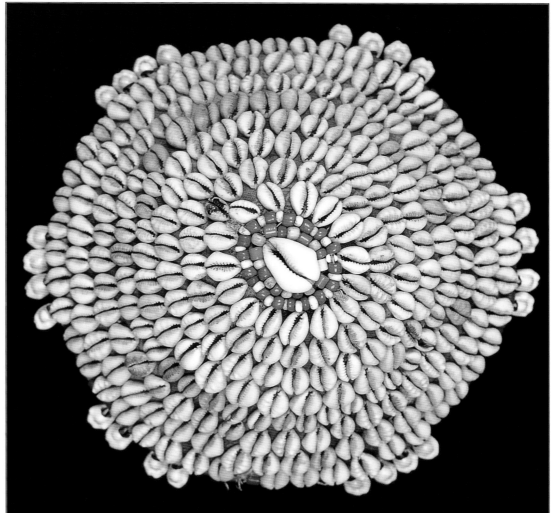

ABOVE AND RIGHT: Top and side views of hat worn by a titled man of the Kuba peoples, Kasai region, Congo in the 20th century. Cowrie shells, blue glass beads, raffia base.

LEFT: Yoruba royal beaded crown, Nigeria. 20th century. Among the Yoruba birds are often a symbol of the mystic powers of women, and one interpretation of the presence of birds on royal crowns is that they demonstrate the ruler has the backing of these powerful and dangerous forces.

LEFT AND ABOVE: *Top and side views of a feather hat worn by* Fon *(kings) and senior dignitaries in various kingdoms of the Grassfields region of Cameroon. The dyed feathers could be folded inside the mesh cap base for convenient storage. 20th century.*

BELOW: *Top and side views of a Zulu married womens'* isicholo *hat woven from ocher-dyed human hair and grass fibers over a basketry frame. Today these hats and similar basketry versions are only worn for ceremonial occasions. The hat is 20th century South African.*

87

ABOVE: Hat known as mpaan, worn by senior Kuba women to denote high titled status, and forming an important component of funeral regalia. It was made in the 20th century, of cowrie shells, beads, cloth, and raffia in the Kasai region of the Congo.

RIGHT: Hat adorned with multi-colored buttons, an idiosyncratic variation on a type worn by Bwami—members of the Lega leadership association—eastern Congo. These hats—this one is 20th century—were worn on top of a flatter cone-shaped raffia cap, itself called bwami, which was buried with its owner.

ABOVE: Lega raffia hat worn by senior grade members of the Bwami association. The polished mussel shells, lubumba, on this hat are reserved for senior initiates and are thought to be associated with femininity and the waxing of the moon. 20th century, eastern Congo.

RIGHT: Feather-adorned mud cap hairpiece of a Pokot man of warrior status. Personal adornment is a key aspect of young men's lives among the pastoralist peoples of Kenya and many hours will be spent on preparing and maintaining these hair decorations.

MASKS AND MASQUERADE

The Makonde, a farming people living along the Mozambique/Tanzania border, are now famous for their ebony sculptures of contorted supernatural figures. A far older local tradition, however, is the elaborate masquerade performances that mark the culmination of a long process by which young boys and girls are initiated into the mysteries of adult life during periods of seclusion in separate camps in the bush. Each masquerader, called *lipoko*, wears a helmet mask carved from light soft wood, over a cloth costume that totally conceals his identity from the crowd of spectators. The masks, carved to resemble a Makonde man or woman, an Arab trader, or even a European, dance through the village accompanied by an orchestra of drummers. Some dancers augment their costume with a further carved wooden body mask, shaped to represent the swollen breasts and belly of a pregnant woman. While to the women and children the masks are supposed to be terrifying beings from the land of the dead, the newly initiated boys share in the secret of the men's masquerade society, having just passed throughan ordeal in which they fought and finally unmasked the performers at the bush camps.

In communities of the Dan people on either side of the border between Liberia and Côte D'Ivoire, young boys who are to be circumcised and initiated into the secrets of manhood are secluded in a camp in the forest, in the past for a period of several months. Each day a friendly forest spirit, in the form of a masquerade called *deangle*, walks gracefully into the village from the camp. Joking and teasing the anxious women whose sons are in the camp, the mask speaking through its small cluster of attendants asks them for the food they have prepared to feed the youths. The mask itself is a small, finely carved, oval of wood, with narrow eyes, slightly pouting lips, and even regular features. Intended to have an attractive feminine look, it may even have been carved as a portrait of a beautiful young woman admired by the sculptor. A band of white chalk across the eyes stands out against the shiny black surface. The masquerader wears a conical headpiece adorned with feathers and cowrie shells, a thick skirt of raffia fibers and a cloak of locally-woven cloth. The deangle is a junior figure in the hierarchy of Dan masquerades. Along with another similar mask that dances for entertainment at festivals, and a third, round-eyed, type used by young men in running races, it is a lesser player in a set of masks which in some villages may comprise as many as eight or ten categories. Other masks dance on stilts or perform magic tricks, while the more serious figures are ferocious forest spirits that, in the past at least, led the community in warfare or sat in judgement over witches and

ABOVE: *The Ebira* eku-ecici *masquerade, a servant of the world of the dead. A woman kneels to request the assistance of the healing power of the ancestors. Photograph taken at Opopocho, Ihima, Nigeria in 1966.*

RIGHT: *Age grade masqueraders of Ogbe, Akoko-Edo area, Nigeria, 1969.*

criminals. Still other masks are never seen, instead simply heard as terrifying cries in the night. All Dan masks are believed to embody powerful spirits from the wild uncultivated bush, that will appear to a man in his dreams, troubling his life until he arranges for a suitable mask to incorporate them. If he is too senior to dance the mask himself, the owner may then select a junior member of his family to be responsible for activating it. Over a period of many years a mask itself may achieve a reputation for successful activity and gradually increase its authority and status almost independently. A men's society known as *go* plays a key role in organizing the performance of the more senior masquerades in a Dan village.

Among the Yoruba of southwestern Nigeria, in many communities a society of men will organize an annual festival at which they will perform a series of masquerades called *Efe/Gelede*. The successful performance of this festival is regarded by its followers as essential to placate the mystical powers of senior women. If they are suitably assuaged these women, known respectfully as "our mothers" or "the owners of birds," will use their powers to the benefit of the community. If offended, however, the negative role of women as witches will come to the fore. Babies will die in the womb, children sicken in infancy, and the prosperity of the town will be spoiled. Despite the widespread adherence to Christianity and Islam, fear of witchcraft is a very real and pervasive concern, as in many other regions of Africa. The performance has its origin in a myth that recounts that *Ifá*, the ancient Yoruba divination system, warned Orunmila, the deity of divination, that he should wear a mask for protection when he went to the forest grove where the witches meet at night.

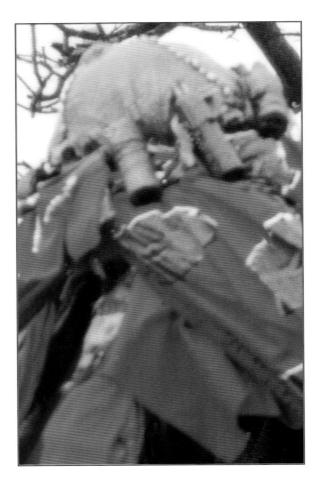

ABOVE (DETAIL) AND RIGHT: *Yoruba Egungun masquerader embodying the spirit of a deceased ancestor, dancing in a celebration of the annual masquerade festival, Oyo, Nigeria, 1995.*

In the night when the festival begins a series of masks appear in the performance space, watched by all the assembled townspeople. The first of two key figures is the Efe mask itself, which sings new and topical songs, often criticizing recent political events and satirizing prominent individuals to much amusement. Although the performer is masked, his identity is not secret, and the success of his performance will be publicly assessed by women as well as men. More serious is a rather mysterious masked figure known as the Great Mother, wearing a white mask headpiece with a huge pointed beak, the tip of which is often stained blood red. This figure seems to embody the feared and respected female power. The Gelede section of the festival takes places the next afternoon and is marked by pairs of dancers with matching masks performing complex choreographed dance moves to the sound of drums and iron rattles. Each mask is a carved helmet shape with a face on the front sitting on top of the dancer's head, while a cloth veil covers his face. On top of the helmet are carved a superstructure of figures of humans or animals involved in any of a huge range of scenes from daily life, novelties, or anything else the carver and maskers hope will attract the eye of the crowd.

However, Gelede is not the only masquerade of the Yoruba. It is only found in the south and southwest, along and across the border between Nigeria and the Republic of Benin. Its range overlaps with that of a very different performance, known as *Egungun* associated with the 17th to early 19th century empire of the Oyo Yoruba. Believed to be the embodiment of ancestral spirits, an important context for these masks is to provide a farewell visit following the death of any senior men in families that belong to the

mask society. A few weeks after the burial a mask will emerge from the dead man's room, dressed in his old clothes, to rebuke any quarreling family members, say farewell to his wives and children, and perhaps accuse someone of responsibility in his death. Other Egungun perform at an annual town festival, parading through the streets with a gang of followers, often surrounded by a posse of excited young men with sticks who chase and beat each other and youths in the crowd. As embodiments of the ancestors, the more important of these masks are thought by many to have healing powers, and often women who are having problems, especially relating to fertility, will kneel and supplicate the spirit for assistance. Small gifts of money are made to the mask's attendants, and if the problem is subsequently resolved a chicken or some other sacrifice may be given. As with the Dan case, certain masks will achieve reputations for successful intercession and may accumulate a growing power, visibly represented on the mask itself by a growing encrustation of black sacrificial residues. Many Egungun are elaborate constructions of different types of cloth, often the most expensive and prestigious velvets and brocades that the owning family could afford. Some, but not all of them, have a wooden headpiece, often in the form of a small head on a tray. In the pre-colonial period certain of the most powerful and fearsome of these Egungun were entrusted with responsibility for dangerous acts of bloodshed such as executing convicted criminals and witches. At the other end of the spectrum however, were masked performers that traveled from town to town doing conjuring tricks and dressing up in fancy costumes to entertain the people.

In previous chapters of this book we have explored some of the ways in which people in different regions of Africa have used aspects of personal adornment to express and embody ideas about a wide variety of concepts including personal and group identity, social status, gender, authority, beauty, fashion, and aesthetics. As the selection of examples we have briefly looked at suggests, masks and masquerading are further means through which some African peoples have used and continue to use their bodies as a medium to construct and display locally important concerns. Although they are often intended to be at least in part a form of entertainment, masks in Africa cannot be seen as simply actors dressing up and performing a role as we have come to understand this process in the European theatrical tradition. Rather they are complex and still powerful phenomena that actively participate in a variety of important aspects of social life. Often they involve troubling and apparently paradoxical reconfigurations of the masker's personal identity, touching on difficult issues of secrecy and local understandings of metaphysical or spiritual agency.

As we have seen masquerades in Africa take a wide variety of different forms and involve a huge range of concerns. This has lead some scholars to question whether we are in fact dealing with a single separate topic, or one that merely appears so to outsiders conditioned by the intellectual history of the ideas of masking in Europe to focus on certain types of activities that involve covering the face while ignoring other related areas. European ideas about masking have two key sources. The terms mask and masquerade are derived from an Arabic verb meaning to mock or make fun, as is the word mascara. The second source is the theatre of ancient Greece and Rome, where actors performed wearing masks that were called persona. From this root evolved ideas relating masks to person and identity. Although these hint at issues which may be involved in African ideas of masquerade as well, we need to ensure that they are actually relevant in specific instances not simply assumed on the basis of the connotations of the words in English. Moreover there are other things going on in Africa, from the veiling of the face by Moslem women, or Tuareg men, to spirit possession, to aspects of body decoration, that may have features in common with the use of masks.

Not all African societies use masks, and contrary to the superficial assumption that they are always ancient traditions, in many that do they have only adopted them over the last century or

RIGHT: Mask headpiece used as one of a pair that dances together as part of a Yoruba Gelede performance intended to placate the mystic powers of women. The double-axe on the crest is in honor of Sango, Yoruba god of thunder and lightning. Southwestern Nigeria, 20th century.

RIGHT: Dan masks worn by Deangle masqueraders who accompany young men to the bush camps for circumcision and initiation into adult status. Liberia, 20th century.

LEFT: 20th century eastern Pende helmet mask from the Kasai region, Congo. Called kipoko, *it was kept in the village chief's house as one of a group of sacred objects directly linked to the welfare of the community. In performance, the masquerade, which can heal the sick, is associated with the transmission of ancestral power.*

RIGHT: 20th century white-faced mask used by the Idoma or neighboring peoples of the Benue river valley, central Nigeria.

so. There can be no doubt however that masquerading has been an important part of the cultural life of many African societies for many centuries. Images interpreted by scholars as masked figures have been found amongst the ancient rock paintings in the Sahara region. The fragmentary remains of a wooden animal head found far to the south in central Angola and carbon dated to around the 8th century, have been tentatively identified as a helmet mask in the form of an aardvark. Nevertheless even in West and Central Africa, where the use of masks is most widespread, there are important groups, such as the Asante of Ghana, that have no masks. Masquerading is not common in the southern part of the continent, while in the east, aside from a few well known instances such as among the Chewa of Malawi and the Makonde of Mozambique and Tanzania, it seems to have declined in popularity in the colonial period. Sometimes this was the result of official prohibitions. In Tanzania for instance the German colonial government banned many men's societies that used to stage masquerades following a rebel-lion in 1905. In areas where masking is practiced it may take on a variety of new meanings and roles as the wider social context has been transformed. Sometimes this has involved masks that were previously of great ritual significance being reduced to acting as secular entertainment, but perhaps equally important has been the spread of masquerades reputed to be effective in combating witchcraft in areas where the upheavals of the 20th century have lead to a loss of faith in older remedies. Although the increasing popularity of Islam and Christianity has led to the abandonment of some masquerade traditions this is by no means always the case. There are even masquerades in some parts of Mali that perform on Islamic festivals such as the end of the Ramadan fast.

The mask itself, usually but not always a carved wooden face covering or headdress, is only a small part of the masquerade costume, let alone of the whole performance. Only the sculptor, or the mask's owner, is likely to see it as the separate object we can display in a museum. The mask in use is part of a cloth or fiber assemblage

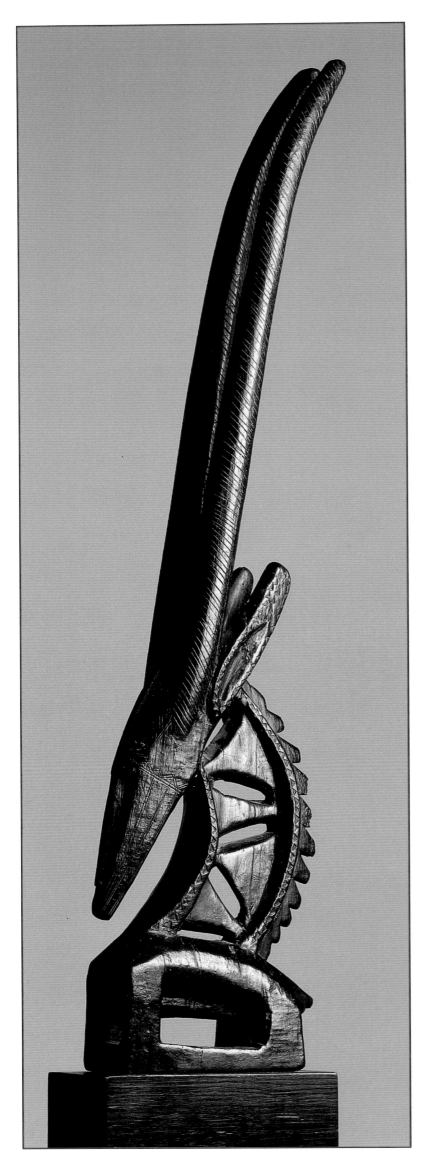

that usually covers the wearer's entire body, often also concealing medicines that can protect the performer against rivals and witches or enhance his dancing skills. Its final appearance involves not just the work of a carver. The mask may be painted by the performer or his colleagues, the cloths making up the outfit contributed by his mother or wives, the final look assessed by a senior official. The collaborative nature of masquerade is even more apparent in performance, which usually involves musicians, often including women singers, interpreters, guards with sticks to control or excite the crowd, and a variety of other attendants. A few masquerades are solo performers, but most will appear in sequence with others as part of an elaborately staged event. It is the process of masquerading and the ideas locally associated with it, rather than the isolated carved wooden artefacts foreigners have collected and admired, that provides clues to an understanding of the phenomenon.

Ideas of spiritual agency are clearly important in many mask events and provide one of the key differences from European theatrical performance. Sometimes, as with the Egungun described above, the spirit involved is thought to be ancestral and therefore, at least in a sense, from within the lineage and within society. More commonly though, the spirits are conceptualized as being from outside the bounds of everyday life in the village or town, usually as spirits of the bush, the forest, or the river. It is noticeable that these are almost always comparatively minor figures in local belief systems and it is very rare for major deities to be represented in mask forms. These spirits are brought from outside, from the wild, into the domain of the village, usually to effect some kind of transformation. Although there are numerous exceptions, it is frequently the case that masquerades perform on occasions that anthropologists have characterized as liminal, that is when individuals or groups are in the process of transition from one stage to another,

LEFT: Chi-wara headdress, representing a fusion of antelope and anteater, danced in pairs to honor champion farmers in Bamana villages, Mali, 20th century.

RIGHT: Dogon kanaga mask, worn by young men in ritual performances known as dama, which serve to transport the souls of the dead away from the village. This one dates from the 20th century and comes from Mali.

perhaps from youths to adults or from elders to ancestors via a funeral. If the masks often effect a social transformation of this kind, they may also involve some kind of transformation in the performers as they are, at least in some instances, considered to have their personal identity temporarily displaced and their body in performance activated by a spirit.

Although virtually no research has been done to explore the perspective of actual maskers, and to understand what it feels like to participate in this potentially disturbing transformation, it is clear that there are complex ideas of secrecy and partial knowledge involved. While on some level the men organizing even the most sacred of masked performances know that there is one of their number actually wearing the mask, it is too simplistic to see this as only a deliberate deceit to fool the gullible women and uninitiated. The evidence suggests that it can be seen both as a trick and an involvement of a very real and powerful spiritual agency at one and the same time. Women watching and interacting with the mask may also know that it is a man dancing, and perhaps even recognize that their husband or brother is the dancer, but still believe that spiritual retribution would follow if they spoke of this knowledge.

As the example of the Yoruba gelede masquerade makes clear, the relationship between men and women is often an important issue that people address and attempt to reconfigure through masked performance. Although masquerades that are in part about women, and male views of the role of women, are not unusual, all the examples of mask use we have discussed so far have been organized, controlled, and worn by men.

Women may play important roles in supporting the performance and interacting with the maskers, but the masks themselves in Africa are in the hands of men. There are numerous cases involving women in practices such as spirit possession, body decoration, and other activities in many ways analogous to aspects of masking, but only one significant area where women themselves cover their faces with wooden masks.

RIGHT: Helmet mask worn during dances accompanying the initiation of boys into adult status among the Makonde of the Tanzania/Mozambique border region. 20th century.

104

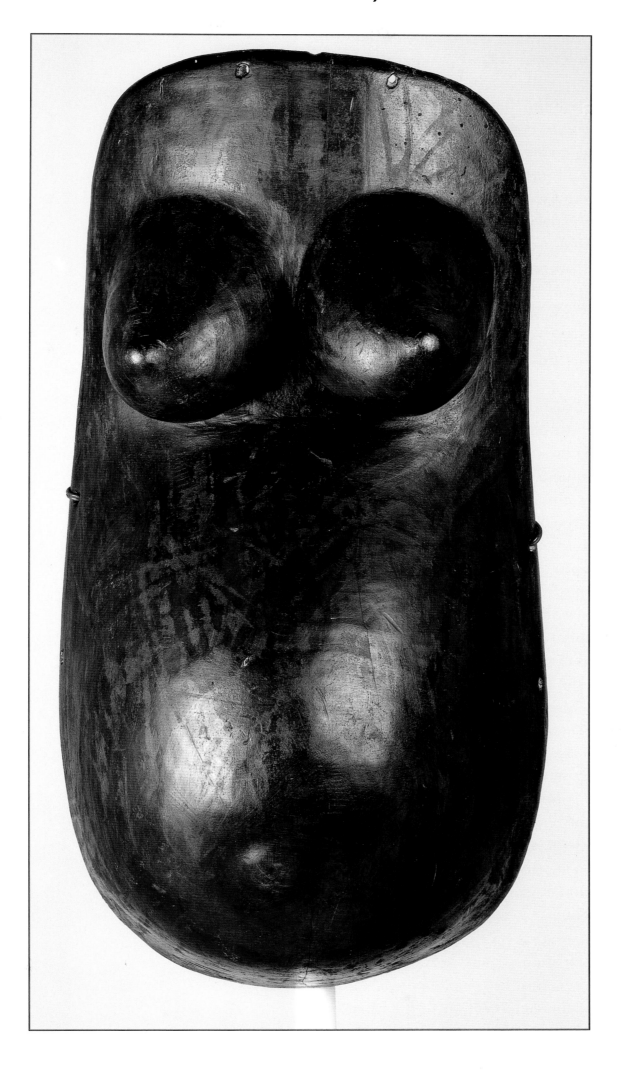

*LEFT AND ABOVE: Helmet mask and body mask worn during
dances accompanying the initiation of boys into adult status
among the Makonde of the Tanzania/Mozambique border region.
20th century.*

Among the Mende, Vai, Sherbro, and neighboring groups in Sierra Leone and Liberia, a women's society, called Sande by the Mende, organizes the training and initiation of young women into socially correct adult status. Sande provides a female counterpart to the local men's society, Poro, and has a number of masquerades that are danced by senior women. The Sande masker, or *sowei*, wears a gleaming black wood helmet mask that usually depicts the idealized beauty of a young woman, complete with elaborately carved depiction of a fashionable hairstyle. It is an important component of a wider set of Mende masks, most others of which are controlled by the Poro group of the men.

It is difficult to provide a satisfactory summary of the incredible diversity of local variations in role of masks in Africa but art historian John Picton has suggested that some aspects can be usefully understood as points along a range between a four-point framework. Many masks, such as that of the Yoruba singer of Efe, appear to be used mainly as devices to create dramatic distance, without necessarily concealing the identity of the performer. Second, there are others, such as the Yoruba ancestral Egungun, that both create dramatic distance and are a means to allow the denial of human agency—in these cases the identity of the masker is "secret" and elaborate rituals are often needed to protect him from the dangers of the supernatural force thought to be involved. In the third group both of these factors are still important, but the actual artefact of the mask itself is believed to contain some spiritual force, either temporarily for the duration of the performance or, as with the Dan example, on a permanent basis. Some masks of royal palace regulatory societies in the Grassfields area of Cameroon become so powerful that it is no longer safe to wear them. Finally there are a number of mask-shaped artefacts, such as the ivory hip ornaments of the Oba or king of Benin, that have no obvious connection to the phenomena of masquerade performance. Detailed investigation of the history and current state of a far

Mask from the Ngunie river region of Gabon, attributed to the Ashira or Punu peoples. Worn by masqueraders dancing on high stilts, they are said to represent the spirits of beautiful young women who return to the village for funerals. 20th century.

wider range of masks in use is necessary before we can make much further progress in assessing their continuing contribution to African societies. They do, however, provide perhaps the most dramatic examples of the importance of the use of the arts of adornment and dress in African societies.

CREDITS

The Author and Publisher gratefully acknowledge the assistance provided by those who lent photographs, jewelry, textiles, and other artefacts for use in this book as acknowledged in the list of page credits below. In particular we'd like to thank Simon Clay for his studio photography and Peter Adler for all the artefacts he provided.

AUTHOR'S COLLECTION
30 (below), 70 (left)

AUTHOR'S PHOTOGRAPH
13 (above), 14, 15, 58 (right), 59, 61, 65 (both), 77, 94, 95

VIA AUTHOR
8, 12, 13 (below), 26, 33, 39 (below left), 42, 50 (above), 56, 58 (left), 72, 75, 76 (both), 78 (both), 82 (both)

PETER ADLER COLLECTION
1, 2, 3, 5, 6/7, 16, 17, 18/19, 22, 23, 24, 25 (both), 27, 28 (both), 29, 30 (above), 31, 34/35, 36, 37, 38, 39 (above and below right), 40 (both), 41, 43, 44/45, 46 (all), 47 (both), 48 (both), 49 (both), 51 (all), 52 (all), 53 (all), 54, 55, 57, 66, 67, 68/69, 71 (both), 73, 74, 81 (both), 83, 84 (both), 85 (both), 86, 87 (all), 88, 89, 90, 91, 97, 98/99, 100, 101, 102, 103, 104/105, 106, 107, 108/109, 110, 111

NIGERIA MAGAZINE VIA AUTHOR
20, 60, 79

E. A. Péri-Willis
9, 10, 11

DR. JOHN PICTON
92, 93